History of the Saints

# THE MORMON WARS

Early Persecutions • Hawn's Mill • The Nauvoo War
War of Extermination • Johnston's Army • The War on Polygamy

GENERAL EDITORS Glenn Rawson and Dennis Lyman

WITH CONTRIBUTIONS BY Mark Staker, William Hartley,
Alexander Baugh, Richard Bennett,
Kenneth Alford, and Thomas Alexander

Covenant Communications, Inc.

Covenant

**Cover images: Top image:** C. C. A. Christensen (1831-1912), *Saints Driven from Jackson County Missouri*, (detail) c.1878, tempera on muslin, 77 1/4 x 113 inches. Brigham Young University Museum of Art, gift of the grandchildren of C.C.A. Christensen, 1970. **Bottom Left:** *Johnston's Army in Echo Canyon* by Edward T. Grigware—courtesy Church History Library. **Bottom Middle:** *Destroying the Press at at Independence* by J. Thompson—courtesy of the LDS Church Archives **Bottom Right:** C. C. A. Christensen (1831-1912), *The Battle of Crooked River*, c.1878, tempera on muslin, 78 x 114 inches. Brigham Young University Museum of Art, gift of the grandchildren of C.C.A. Christensen, 1970. **Front Flap:** *Leaving Missouri* by CCA Christensen—courtesy of Brigham Young University Museum of Art. All rights reserved. **Back Flap:** C. C. A. Christensen (1831-1912), *Leaving Missouri*, c.1878, tempera on muslin, 78 1/8 x 114 1/8 inches. Brigham Young University Museum of Art, gift of the grandchildren of C.C.A. Christensen, 1970.

Cover and interior design copyright © 2014 by Covenant Communications, Inc.

Published by Covenant Communications, Inc.
American Fork, Utah

Printed in China
First Printing: April 2014

20 19 18 17 16 15 14    10 9 8 7 6 5 4 3 2 1

ISBN 978-1-62108-716-8

# TABLE OF CONTENTS

# WAR ON THE SAINTS
## "The Adversary Was Aware":
### The Beginnings of Persecution in New York, Pennsylvania, and Ohio

MARK L. STAKER

## NEW YORK

In the opening decades of the nineteenth century, even an unnoticed boy raised in Vermont's isolated green mountains knew about the persecution of early Christians and had heard stories of lions, gladiators, and defiant martyrs. Yet when the mature Joseph Smith reflected on the experiences of his youth, he still expressed surprise that some of those he trusted most would persecute him. They were "men of high standing," he recalled. Joseph noted that persecution arose against him "almost in my infancy," and, he surmised, "It seems as though the adversary was aware, at a very early period of my life, that I was destined to prove a disturber and an annoyer of his kingdom" (JS—H 1:20).

When Joseph was fourteen years old, shortly after his family had moved to western New York, he experienced a remarkable vision, the sharing of which contributed to his sense of persecution. He recalled years later rehearsing "an account of the vision" he recently had with a minister active in his community; Joseph noted that the trusted man responded "with great contempt." Soon young Joseph found that having told this story "excited a great deal of prejudice against me among professors of religion, and was the cause of great persecution, which continued to increase" as "men of high standing" and "the great ones" began to take notice (JS—H 1:21–23). No wonder Joseph was reluctant to share the details of his remarkable vision. He may have even kept the principal elements of his experience from his own family, since those supposedly most spiritually attuned in the area rejected him. He related telling his mother after the vision simply that he had learned her religion "was not true," while

In the spring of 1820, Joseph Smith saw the Father and the Son. Opening the heavens after ages of apostasy and bringing light to the faithful, this vision also stirred up wrath and persecution against Joseph.

Moroni visited seventeen-year-old Joseph Smith in September 1823. Because of Joseph's reluctance to share his experiences with others, Moroni had to command Joseph to tell his father about his visions.

also recalling he "could find none that would believe the hevnly [heavenly] vision."[1]

Three years later, Joseph had another remarkable spiritual experience when an angel who identified himself as Moroni appeared to the youth during the night of September 21–22, 1823. One of the first things the angel did was to put Joseph's recent persecution in context. Moroni called him by name and informed Joseph that his "name should be had for good and evil among all nations, kindreds, and tongues, or that it should be both good and evil spoken of among all people" (JS—H 1:33).

In the morning, Joseph said nothing of his experiences, presumably planning to follow his earlier approach, until Moroni visited him again in the family apple orchard and "commanded me to go to my father and tell him of the vision and commandments which I had received" (JS—H 1:49). He obeyed. His younger brother William, apparently unaware of Joseph's earlier recounting of the experience to a trusted minister, remembered working in the fields next to him the morning after Moroni's repeated visits when the boy prophet invited him along with the rest of the family into "his father's house together and communicate[d] to them the visions he had received, which he had not yet told to any one."[2] As Joseph related his remarkable visions, "the whole family were melted to tears, and believed all he said." Finally, after Joseph had experienced what he perceived as "great persecution" from religious leaders and others he trusted implicitly, he now found some would hold his name for good and believe him—his own family. While persecution continued to increase, from that point on Joseph would always have a small group of followers who supported and sustained him. This made the persecution bearable but brought abuse on those he loved as well.

Eight months after Joseph married Emma Hale, the two of them went to the large hill near his home after midnight on September 22, 1827, and under the darkness of night Joseph retrieved the golden plates placed there by the angel while Emma stayed by the carriage and prayed for his success. Soon some neighbors pressed to see the plates while others tried to steal the plates, and Joseph's family was quickly drawn into helping him protect them. Joseph's younger sister Catherine recalled in later years how as a young girl she was home when her brother arrived out of breath with the plates wrapped in a cloth. "He was carrying the package clasped to his side with his left hand and arm, and his right hand was badly bruised from knocking down at least three men who had leaped at him." Catherine quickly helped him hide the plates, which "were very heavy," and she then treated Joseph's injuries.[3]

While constantly protecting the plates and trying to keep his family safe, Joseph faced the jeers, verbal abuse, and physical attacks that accompanied his persecution. Virtually everyone in Wayne County, New York—where Joseph lived—had heard of the golden plates, and the accompanying persecution made it difficult for Joseph to translate them. He recognized it was sometimes easier to avoid persecution altogether than to constantly defend against it. His brother William recalled, "a great persecution arose against the whole family, and [Joseph] was compelled to remove into Pennsylvania."[4]

No sooner did Joseph get possession of the plates than others resorted to every stratagem imaginable to take them from him.

## PENNSYLVANIA

Joseph and Emma loaded all they owned into a small farm wagon driven by Emma's brother Alva Hale, who took them down the turnpike to the Isaac and Elizabeth Hale family farm in Harmony, Pennsylvania, where they arrived in December 1827. Before leaving, Joseph nailed the golden plates into a wooden box, covered the box with beans in a partly empty barrel, and sealed the barrel closed before putting it in the wagon for the trip. Alva, who was the local elected constable in Harmony Township,[5] provided protection for the plates as the trio traveled from Wayne County, New York, to northeastern Pennsylvania's Susquehanna Valley, where Joseph would begin translation of the Book of Mormon.

Emma's father, Isaac, recalled that soon after the couple arrived at his home, "I was informed they had brought a

wonderful book of Plates down with them. I was shown a box in which it is said they were contained." When Isaac Hale learned, however, that he could not then see the plates, he insisted of Joseph, "if there was anything in my house of that description, which I could not be allowed to see, he must take it away; if he did not, I was determined to see it."[6] Joseph then kept the plates hidden in the woods to protect them until he and Emma moved into their own home shortly before Martin Harris came to assist Joseph as a scribe.

Although Joseph found a brief respite in Pennsylvania from inquiring and pressing New York neighbors, the move brought its own challenges as Emma's brothers and her cousins soon began to chide him. During the translation process Emma's family would sometimes stop and yell rude comments through the front doorway, as the door was left open to circulate air during the hot summer. Joseph went fishing on the Susquehanna River with Emma's relatives until an attempt to defend himself against their irascible comments led to blows.

On June 26, 1830, Joseph's friend Newel Knight helped others dam a small stream near the Knight home in Colesville, Broome County, New York, twenty miles north of Joseph's Pennsylvania home. This created a small pond of water for a Sunday baptismal service the following morning. Newel later recalled, "There were many in our neighborhood who believed, and were anxiously waiting for an opportunity to be baptized."[7] Toward the end of a hot June, the spring freshets were gone and the Susquehanna River that ran along the Knight property was back to its typical one-foot-

Persecution seemed to follow Joseph everywhere he went. When he and Emma came to Harmony, Pennsylvania, he hoped to have uninterrupted peace to translate. That proved not to be the case, however, and some of Emma's family members were among his chief persecutors.

Colesville, New York—like Harmony, Pennsylvania—also lay along the beautiful Susquehanna River. It was home to the Knight family, friends of the Prophet Joseph who were subjected to some of the same persecution that came upon him.

deep levels. This made the growing pond the only available water for baptisms by immersion in the area, and during the night some of the local citizens, urged on by "certain sectarian priests of the neighborhood," breached the pond's dam, thinking they could keep their neighbors from getting baptized. Despite the lack of a proper facility in the morning, Oliver Cowdery still preached a sermon on the principles of repentance, baptism, and laying on of hands for the gift of the Holy Ghost to an attentive audience, inviting his listeners to commit to baptism. His words apparently touched a number of hearts, since that evening some of the men repaired the dam, and early Monday morning the small group of believers had enough water in a small pond that they baptized at least twelve converts before angry neighbors had time to gather. Although the neighbors ridiculed the new converts and mocked those who performed the baptisms, asking them if they "had been washing sheep," the small congregation of the Church of Christ resolutely continued their meeting.[8]

Confirmations at that time frequently took place near the water's edge, but, perhaps to avoid confrontation by the gathering crowd, the congregation scheduled a confirmation meeting for later that evening. As the evening meeting approached, a constable from neighboring Chenango County arrived with a warrant to arrest and try Joseph Smith as a "disorderly person" in that county. The constable took Joseph from Colesville, Broome County, to South Bainbridge, where he had been tried and acquitted of being

It was near Pickerel Pond, pictured here, that the creek was dammed for baptisms; a mob subsequently tore the dam down.

a disorderly person four years earlier.[9] This time the circulation of "scandalous falsehoods" about him attracted a boisterous crowd that gathered, anxious to see the proceedings. The constable had to sleep in the same room with Joseph that night with a loaded gun by his side and his feet firmly pressed against the door to assure Joseph's safety until the trial could begin the next day.

Joseph Knight Sr. hired two local farmers, James Davidson and John S. Reid, to help with Joseph Smith's defense as the prosecution scoured the county for witnesses who had heard anything "which could be made a pretext against Joseph."[10] No one was able to say anything of consequence. The person in the county who knew Joseph best, Josiah Stowell, testified in court, "I am well acquainted with Joseph Smith, Jun., and know him to be honest."[11] The judge acquitted Joseph.

At "the very moment" the court released Joseph, a constable from Broome County arrested him again on the same charge. This constable refused to allow Joseph to eat, even though the twenty-four-year-old had been in court all day and had not eaten anything since morning. The constable hurried Joseph off to the town of Colesville while giving insults and abuse. When they arrived at the local tavern, men gathered around Joseph to ridicule and insult him. Joseph later recalled, "They spit upon me, pointed their fingers at me, saying, 'Prophesy, prophesy!' and thus did they imitate those who crucified the Savior of mankind, not knowing what they did."

The next morning two local farmers, William Seymour and Amasa Burch, argued for the prosecution, while the two farmers defending Joseph in South Bainbridge came to Colesville to repeat their defense and "spoke like men inspired of God." The court again acquitted Joseph of the charges. When Joseph was finally free, he went to the nearby home of Emma's sister and her husband, Elizabeth and Benjamin Wasson, where Emma had stayed with other members of the Church who gathered to pray and wait. Emma cried with joy as she saw her husband coming toward her.

Joseph and Emma returned safely to their home in Harmony, Pennsylvania, but Joseph still needed to confirm those who had been baptized in Colesville because the persecution had not allowed them to complete that priesthood ordinance.

In a letter dated August 29, 1830, Joseph explained that he could not return to Colesville because of persecution.

Knowing the bitter animosity expressed by some people in Colesville and the surrounding villages of Broome County, there was a natural concern for Joseph's safety if he were to travel the twenty miles north to the Colesville Branch and minister to their needs. But the Prophet determined to return north anyway and make sure the confirmations were carried out.

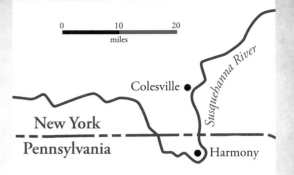

John and David Whitmer joined Joseph and Hyrum Smith as they prayed God would make it so their enemies could not see them so that "on this occasion they might return unmolested." As the four men traveled along the turnpike toward Colesville, their only route seemed blocked—in front of them they saw oxen pulling graders along the road and a large company of men wielding picks, sledge hammers, and shovels leveling out the ground, a duty required by law each year of every able-bodied man in the community. As they drew closer, the men could see some of the bitterest opponents of the newly organized Church among the road crew. While the workers shouted out directions to the oxen, sang songs to keep rhythm as they labored, and clanged their tools against the rough road, Joseph and his companions quietly moved alongside them on the edge of the road and slowly passed them. The workmen looked up from their labor and did not seem to recognize Joseph, Hyrum, John, or David, even though some of the road crew had offered a reward to anyone giving information about Joseph's return to the area. The seemingly invisible men spent that evening with the Saints in Colesville, where they confirmed new members and partook of the sacrament together unmolested.

It was while traveling along the road from Harmony to Colesville that Joseph and others were miraculously hidden from the sight of their enemies.

Despite the protection Joseph and his associates enjoyed "on this occasion," persecution in the area continued unabated so that it became impossible for them to continue to minister to the needs of their followers from the Susquehanna Valley. Joseph had remodeled and expanded the size of his Pennsylvania home dramatically so that it could accommodate the headquarters of the Church had he wished,[12] but Joseph and Emma were forced to leave their home behind in September 1830, and Emma would never again see her parents or the valley where she was born and raised.

# OHIO

On October 28, 1830, Parley P. Pratt and Oliver Cowdery walked into the small village of Mentor, Ohio, about twenty-five miles northeast of Cleveland on the edge of Lake Erie, lugging along a satchel full of newly bound copies of the Book of Mormon; at the same time, their missionary companions, Ziba Peterson and Peter Whitmer, were in the nearby village of Euclid preaching from the same book. The missionaries' initial Mentor efforts were not well received. They handed a copy of their book to the local minister, Sidney Rigdon, who "partly condemned it" but allowed them to preach a sermon in his church the following day. Afterward, the companions left town hungry with no converts and little encouragement.

Meanwhile, the two missionaries in Euclid preached to an attentive audience that included Isaac Morley from nearby Kirtland. During the next week a large number of settlers in and around Kirtland, Ohio, joined the Church. Among the early converts were Sophia Howe, the wife of local newspaperman Eber D. Howe, and his sisters Harriet Howe and the Widow Hutt. Eber Howe had recently announced his retirement from the printing business; had sold his newspaper, the *Painesville Telegraph*; and had planned to devote himself to other activities. But after his family joined "the work," as they referred to the new religion, Howe noted "circumstances have rendered it necessary that I should again resume the charge of the *Telegraph*," and he came out of retirement to dedicate the full resources of his publishing toward stopping what he called "the Mormonites."[13] This short, thickly muscled, big-boned newspaper editor became one of the leading figures in the war against the Latter-day

In a revelation given to the Prophet Joseph Smith in October 1830, Parley P. Pratt, Ziba Peterson, Oliver Cowdery, and Peter Whitmer Jr. were called on a mission to the Lamanites. This mission would lead to numerous conversions and the establishment of a branch of the Church in the area of Kirtland, Ohio. The revelation would become D&C 32.

Saints as he continued to publish newspaper articles ridiculing the Book of Mormon and newly received revelations.

Howe eventually published *Mormonism Unvailed* (sic), the first full-length book attacking the Latter-day Saints. This1834 volume included an extensive attack on the Book of Mormon by Howe himself; an extensive attack on Joseph Smith through a collection of affidavits gathered by an excommunicated member, Doctor Philastus Hurlbut; and an attack on Church members and their proceedings through a series of letters written by Ezra Booth. The Ezra Booth letters had already helped solidify antagonism toward Church members when first published in a local newspaper.

The well-educated Ezra Booth had come from New Haven, Connecticut, to rural Ohio, preaching Methodism as early as 1817. His unusually large head was seen as expressive of his equally unusually large amount of knowledge on history and other subjects. In March 1831 one of Booth's parishioners, Lyman Johnson, came home to Hiram, Ohio, with a copy of the Book of Mormon. Booth, as his minister, stayed up late into the evening with Lyman and Lyman's parents, John and Elsa Johnson, reading and discussing passages from the book. They decided together the book was probably true and Joseph was a prophet.

Lyman's mother, Elsa Johnson, had an afflicted right arm, and the group agreed they would go to Kirtland to ask Joseph Smith to heal her. Ezra Booth; his wife, Dorcas; several members of the Johnson family; and a local doctor all went to Kirtland, where they crowded into the small front parlor of the Whitney home. Joseph blessed Elsa, and she was miraculously healed. Booth was baptized shortly afterward. "When I embraced Mormonism," he recalled, "I conscientiously believed it to be of God. The impressions of my mind were deep and powerful, and my feelings were excited to a degree to which I had been a stranger. . . . [A]t times I was much elated."[14]

Soon after Booth was baptized, he was called to serve a mission. He found the call difficult to accept and acknowledged, "I hesitated for a while."[15] Booth then went on his mission, walking the whole way to Missouri as commanded,

MORMONISM UNVAILED:
OR,
A FAITHFUL ACCOUNT OF THAT SINGULAR IMPOSITION AND
DELUSION,
FROM ITS RISE TO THE PRESENT TIME.
WITH SKETCHES OF THE CHARACTERS OF ITS
PROPAGATORS,
AND A FULL DETAIL OF THE MANNER IN WHICH THE FAMOUS
GOLDEN BIBLE
WAS BROUGHT BEFORE THE WORLD.
TO WHICH ARE ADDED,
INQUIRIES INTO THE PROBABILITY THAT THE HISTORICAL PART
OF THE SAID BIBLE WAS WRITTEN BY ONE
SOLOMON SPALDING,
MORE THAN TWENTY YEARS AGO, AND BY HIM INTENDED TO HAVE
BEEN PUBLISHED AS A ROMANCE.
BY E. D. HOWE.
PAINESVILLE:
PRINTED AND PUBLISHED BY THE AUTHOR.
1834.

Eber D. Howe, an anti-Mormon newspaper editor, published this first full-length book against the Church. He relied heavily on the written attacks of Ezra Booth, an apostate.

traveling without purse or scrip, forcing both him and his companion to assume "the appearance and [be] justly entitled to the character of beggars."[16] As Booth prepared to return from his mission, he and his associates were commanded by revelation to preach on the way and not return in haste (see D&C 60:8). But he and his companion opted to head for home, using a steamboat and stagecoach. "It is true," Booth acknowledged, "[that] we violated the commandment by not preaching by the way. . . . But it seems that none of us considered the commandment worthy of much notice."[17]

By the time he returned to his home in Ohio, Booth had lost his testimony. He came out in open opposition against the Church with the collusion of his good friend and fellow minister, Ira Eddy. Booth wrote a letter attacking Mormonism, and Eddy took that letter to the local newspaper editor, Lewis Rice, who published it in the middle of page five of his paper without editorial comment. The letter was an immediate sensation. Booth quickly wrote eight more. His letters were soon moved from the back pages to the front page and were given full attention by the newspaper's editor and the general public. Other newspapers copied the letters, which gave them wide circulation throughout the country, and they were read with interest.

Although the letters were negative, they distributed information about the Church widely, resulting in many people hearing about it for the first time. Some people who might otherwise not have heard from the missionaries read the letters

Ezra Booth and others were called by revelation on a mission to Missouri; Booth would serve that mission but would become disaffected and disgruntled by the experience. He returned to Ohio and took up the pen against the Church. This revelation became D&C 52.

and wanted more information. Ira Ames was one of these. He was living in New York at the time and recalled: "When reading his [Booth's] letters, I felt an impression that there was something to Mormonism. There was considerable talk about it in the neighborhood."[18] He joined the Church a few months later.

Shortly after his own conversion, Ezra Booth had preached in Hiram, Ohio, and baptized a local apple farmer, Symonds Ryder, the hamlet's Disciple of Christ lay preacher. The tall, thin, and wiry Ryder became troubled by a revelation given shortly before Booth left for Missouri to serve a mission. Ryder read in the revelation that members were commanded to "consecrate all thy properties, that which thou hast unto me . . . and they shall be laid before the bishop of my church" (Book of Commandments 44:26). Ryder published the text of the revelation on September 6, 1831, in the first printed attack on the Church by a former member. He apparently expected the revelation to influence his neighbors as negatively as it had him, but it had little immediate impact. The following February, however, public opinion began to shift, and Ryder was again influential in the community.

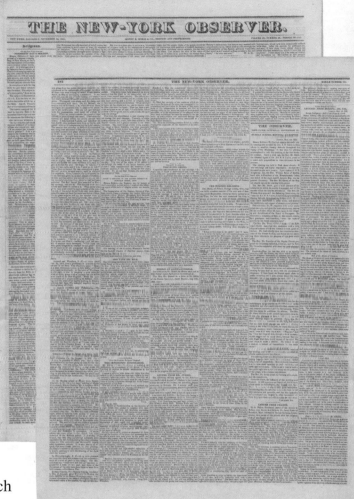

Under the date of November 12, 1831, the *New York Observer* carried one of Ezra Booth's letters against the Church.

## A BRUTAL ATTACK ON JOSEPH SMITH AND SIDNEY RIGDON

February 16, 1832, opened in Hiram, Ohio, with deep snow and temperatures well below freezing. During that day, Joseph Smith and Sidney Rigdon continued their translation of the Bible with a number of observers in the room watching them as they worked. The two men were at a table in an upper room of the John and Elsa Johnson home, where they sat next to a window that provided light by which they could read and write on an overcast day. As they worked, they experienced a vision that lasted "for hours" and was later partly written down in what has since become Section 76 of the Doctrine and Covenants. They were directed to keep the revelation secret for a time, probably because of the disruption it would eventually cause, but it spread by word of mouth anyway. Sidney Rigdon later recalled, "It was at this time we sat for hours in the Visions of heaven around the throne of God & gazed upon the scenes of Eternity. . . . Afterwards the mob came in & broke the door, took me & dragged me out through the streets . . . This is the reason why we were in secret under lock & key."[19]

This vision introduced what Brigham Young, one of Joseph Smith's close associates, described as "new doctrine to this generation," including what he termed the idea that "the Lord was going to save everybody." Brigham Young added that "many stumbled at it."[20]

As news of the revelation spread by missionaries and others, many members in Hiram and the surrounding villages were also preparing to go to "Zion" and begin to build a righteous society in western Missouri.

John and Elsa Johnson were prosperous farmers living near Hiram, Ohio. After the healing of Sister Johnson's arm, the Johnsons invited Joseph and Emma to come and live with them. The Johnsons even gave up their own room to the newcomers to make them feel welcome.

Eleven days after receiving their marvelous vision, Joseph Smith and Sidney Rigdon joined others in a meeting at the Johnson home to "arrange for a great day in the following Spring" when a large group of more than a hundred members would leave for Missouri.[21] While at the meeting, they were given "notice that they would be mobbed." Although no one recorded what this "notice" was, it apparently included threats delivered in person since, in a scene reminiscent of an encounter recorded in the Book of Mormon between Nephi and his brothers Laman and Lemuel (see 1 Ne. 17:48–55), Joseph "dared anyone to touch a Mormon saying that anyone who should do so would be stricken by the Lord."[22] The results also paralleled the Book of

Mormon encounter as the meeting ended with a few angry individuals backing down.

The respite proved only temporary.[23] The combination of members and their families who were troubled by the new doctrine found in the vision—and non-members who had relatives preparing to leave them—"ripened into open war." "Someone bored an auger-hole into the house in which Rigdon lived, and filling it with powder, tried to blow up the cabin."[24] The Rigdon family with its six small children was undoubtedly terrified by this attack, which added to the stress of the children who were "then sick with the measles."[25]

Joseph and Julia Murdock, the adopted eleven-month-old twin infants of Joseph and Emma, also had severe cases of the measles.[26] On Saturday, March 24, 1832, the weary parents went to bed early, caring for their two sick infants. Vermont settlers considered measles a serious affliction that required a warm room, hot baths, and steam. The work kitchen at the rear of the Johnson home with its cistern and water pump provided all of the necessary elements doting parents needed to care for their sick children, although the humid setting may have

It was while translating the Bible on the second floor of the Johnson home that Joseph and Sidney received the revelation now known as D&C 76. Ironically, this revelation, so filled with heavenly light, would anger people to the point of murder.

made the parents restless during the night. Emma, who was six weeks pregnant, awoke to find her husband, Joseph, up with the infant boy and asked him to lie down on the trundle bed that was pulled out near the door from underneath the main bed. He quickly fell asleep.

While Joseph slept, about twenty-five men gathered at Benjamin Hinkley's brickyard a little more than half a mile east of the Johnson home to drink and build up their courage. Symonds Ryder was captain of the local militia and may have been a leader of the men, but the children of Silas Raymond, an ensign in the same militia, claimed he led the group.[27] Men had gathered from surrounding towns as well, and the group likely included people beyond the influence of any one individual. After the men blackened their faces, they divided into two groups and quietly marched west. One company of men reached the Rigdon cabin across the road from the Johnson house and "broke the door," rushed into the room, and in the dark dragged Vashti Higley, a woman helping care for the sick children, from her bed. After they discovered their error, the men went back in and found Sidney and Phebe Rigdon in another room.[28] Sidney later recalled, "I was dragged out of my bed. . . . My head went thump thump upon the hard frozen ground—they then threw a quantity of pitch upon me."[29] He was put on a large pile of wood, where they attacked him and tried to throw nitric acid on him to burn his skin before covering him in tar pitch.

Meanwhile Joseph was soundly sleeping in the rear of the Johnson home across the road. Emma was awake in the darkness and could hear a muffled sound but ignored it until a group of men "burst open the door" and pushed into the room in an instant. The men surrounded the trundle bed where Joseph slept and grabbed him quickly, carrying him outside so fast that by the time the tired father awoke he was already out the door. Joseph "made a desperate struggle," and someone pulled a handful of his hair out by the roots, leaving a permanent bald spot he would hide years later by the way he combed his hair.[30]

Joseph managed during the struggle to loosen one leg; he used it to kick local strongman and farmer Warren Waste in the face so hard that he knocked Waste off the stoop and "sent him sprawling in the street" that ran back to the barn along the west side of the home. The men regrouped and held Joseph firmly as they "passed around the house" with him to the main road in front. They stopped briefly as someone tried to strangle Joseph until he briefly fainted.

When Joseph revived, the mob took him east about five hundred feet. In the moonlight he could see Sidney Rigdon already stretched out on a wood pile looking as though he were dead. The men had not coordinated well where they would meet after grabbing their victims, since the original planned site was now already taken by those attacking Rigdon; the group took Joseph another five hundred feet south into a meadow, where they began to scratch and paw him. The dynamics of the

men were such that everyone seemed to have different ideas. One man—Joseph thought it was Symonds Ryder—was concerned about Joseph catching cold and requested the others keep him off the frozen ground.[31] Someone suggested castrating him. Others argued they should kill him.[32] Joseph, overhearing the discussion, responded, "You will have mercy and spare my life, I hope."[33]

Richard Dennison, a local doctor who was frail and thin and not able to do much physical harm, was one of those who had planned murder and showed no mercy. He brought some nitric acid used in his medical practice—a substance that would horribly burn the esophagus and lead to a coma followed by death. When someone tried to thrust a paddle of tar into Joseph's mouth, Dennison tried to force the acid in as well, but most of it spilled onto Joseph's face, badly burning his skin. The attempt to open his mouth was done with such violence that one of Joseph's upper teeth was completely broken out, leaving a gaping reminder of the incident.[34] As the men scratched, hit, and kicked Joseph, they also severely injured his side, possibly breaking a rib, so that it was still tender years later.[35] But the lack of organization placed the efforts of the men at odds as "the mob became divided, and did not succeed."[36]

The men were unsuccessful in killing Joseph largely because of divine intervention more than any other factor. Heber C. Kimball, one of Joseph Smith's close associates, related that the mob did kill the Prophet during the attack but his spirit returned to his body. "I heard him say himself," Heber recalled, that Joseph's spirit returned "when they killed his body and his spirit was in the heavens looking down upon his body and [he] saw the mob pouring aquafortis [nitric acid] down his neck."[37] Frederick Kesler, an early bishop in Utah, explained that Joseph's spirit "left his body, and hovered over it in the

It was early on Sunday, March 25, 1832, that a mob under the cover of darkness broke into the Johnson home and took Joseph. Before they were through, they had brutally beaten him and had tarred and feathered him.

Frederick Kesler testified that Joseph's spirit left his body when he was tarred and feathered. In short, the mob killed him.

March 25, 1832, was a Sunday, and notwithstanding being bruised and scarred from the events of the night before, Joseph preached "the principles of the gospel" and baptized three people.

air, and returned after it was over. They supposed they had killed him, but he had to come back and take his body."[38]

As the men attacked Joseph, they heard a noise and fled in fear, leaving him alone. As he stood up in the darkness, Joseph could see a light in the distance at the Johnson home and slowly made his way there along the road. He stumbled to the house wearing nothing but the tar and feathers given him by the mob. Emma fainted as others threw a blanket to Joseph and then helped him into the house, where they cleaned the Prophet so he could deliver the Sunday morning sermon in a few hours at the local schoolhouse.[39]

Twelve-year-old Katherine Hulet was touched during the subsequent schoolhouse meeting as she listened to Joseph. There he stood in front of a congregation that included some of the men who had attacked him the night before. His face still showed acid burns on his skin, there was a fresh hole between his teeth, and there were other obvious injuries from the brutal attack. He had also been up all night dealing with a sick child, the mob, and the clean-up. But young Katherine still felt the Spirit as Joseph stood there and meekly taught "the principles of the gospel" to a largely attentive audience.[40] After he finished his sermon, Joseph baptized three members of the congregation in the small stream west of the Johnson home.

A few days after the brutal attack on Joseph Smith and Sidney Rigdon, the infant Joseph Murdock died—one of the first casualties

of growing persecution. The continued blows to Rigdon's head were severe and apparently led him to behave in erratic and illogical ways for several weeks after the attack; he never seemed to be quite the same again.[41] Joseph recognized as a result of the attack that he was vulnerable and could be killed. After that, he always tried to have a bodyguard with him for additional protection.

Joseph moved his family to Kirtland in September 1832. This move did not stop opposition; in fact, the opposition seemed to increase. The following year, as members of the Church started building the Kirtland Temple, they found they had to guard the building with loaded guns at night to keep the walls from being torn down. When the Latter-day Saints tried to create a financial institution to aid the poor in gathering to Kirtland and in financing city growth, they were confronted by outsiders who sought to destroy the institution and threatened its members.[42]

Finally, on January 12, 1838, Joseph Smith received a revelation that directed the "Presidency of my Church" to take their families as soon as possible and flee to Missouri for safety. Six months later, after many Church leaders had fled for Missouri, "Kirtland Camp" formed with 515 Latter-day Saints, their wagons, their animals, and their supplies. On July 6, 1838, this group left Ohio on the way to Zion in western Missouri. They left miraculously "without an enemy to oppose us."[43] As they headed south out of town in the heat of the day, "citizens both males & females stood in their doors and windows and heard our songs."[44] Although the Saints had to flee persecution once again, they remained optimistic and committed.

Another tragic result of the assault of March 25 was that Joseph Murdock, one of the twins Emma had been given to raise, took sick; within days, he passed away—making him, an innocent child, a martyr.

Once again persecutions forced Joseph and the faithful to flee. It was January 1838 when Joseph received a revelation commanding him to flee Kirtland and go to Missouri.

Bottom: January 12, 1838, Revelation to Joseph Smith and the First Presidency—courtesy of the Church History Library

# Endnotes

1   Karen Lynn Davidson, David J. Whittaker, Mark Ashurst-McGee, and Richard Jensen, *Joseph Smith Histories, 1832–1844, The Joseph Smith Papers*, vol. 1 (Salt Lake City: The Church Historian's Press, 2012), 13. I am indebted to Donald L. Enders, Master Curator (retired), Historic Sites Division, LDS Church History Department, for first making me aware many years ago of Joseph's reticence to tell his own family of his First Vision experience.

2   William Smith, *William Smith on Mormonism: A True Account of the Origin of the Book of Mormon* (Lamoni, IA: Herald Steam Book and Job Office, 1883), 9. William was twelve years old when Joseph gathered the family together and told them about his experiences, and he may have later confused some of the elements of that account—recalling that it was an angel who appeared to Joseph and told him his sins were forgiven him and that none of the sects were right. But William would remember when he first became aware of his brother's spiritual experiences.

3   H. S. Salisbury, Transcription of Dictograph Interview with I. B. Bell, LDS Archives MS 4134; H. S. Salisbury, "Memories of Grandmother Catherine S. Salisbury, June 30, 1945," LDS Archives MS 4122–2; Emma M. Phillips, *Dedicated to Serve: Biographies of 31 Women of the Restoration* (Independence, MI: Herald House, 1970), 11–12.

4   William Smith, *William Smith on Mormonism*, 11. One of Joseph's neighbors partly dismissed what his sister and other residents did in relation to the Smith family but agreed Joseph was forced to move "to avoid what he called persecution." Willard Chase, "Affidavit," *Mormonism Unvailed*, E. D. Howe, ed. (Painesville, OH: E. D. Howe, 1834), 246.

5   Alva Hale was elected and duly sworn in as constable on several occasions, including the period during which Joseph Smith worked on the Book of Mormon translation; see "Returned to the Court as Elected Township and Burough [sic] Officers for the Ensuing Year," Harmony Township, Quarter Sessions Docket Book, Susquehanna County, Vol. 3, 1824–1832, Susquehanna County Courthouse, Montrose, Pennsylvania.

6   Isaac Hale, Affidavit, *Mormonism Unvailed*, E. D. Howe, ed. (Painesville, OH: E. D. Howe, 1834), 264.

7   Newel Knight, "Newel Knight Journal," *Scraps of Biography. Tenth Book of the Faith-Promoting Series* (Salt Lake City: Juvenile Instructor Office, 1883), 53.

8   Joseph Knight Jr. "Names of the First Six Members of the Church, Statement, 1862, August 11," Joseph Knight, Jr. File, MS 286 fd. 3., LDS Church Archives, Salt Lake City, Utah.

9   Gordon A. Madsen, "Joseph Smith's 1826 Trial: The Legal Setting," *BYU Studies* 30, no. 2 (1990): 91–108.

10  Newel Knight, 57.

11  Newel Knight, 56–57.

12  See forthcoming article by the author in *Mormon Historical Studies*.

13  Mark Staker, *Hearken, O Ye People: The Historical Setting of Joseph Smith's Ohio Revelations* (Salt Lake City: Greg Kofford Books, 2010), 71–74.

14  E. D. Howe, ed., *Mormonism Unvailed* (Painesville, OH: E. D. Howe, 1834), 176.

15  Ezra Booth, "Mormonism, VII, November 21, 1831," *Ohio Star* 2, no. 47 (November 24, 1831): 1.

16  Ibid.

17  Ibid.

18  Ira Ames, Autobiography and Journal, 1858. MS 6055. Microfilm of holograph. LDS Church History Library, 6.

19  Thomas Bullock, Minutes of April Conference, Nauvoo, Illinois, April 6, 1844, spelling modernized. See also Scott G. Kenney, ed., *Wilford Woodruff's Journal, 1833-1898* (Midvale, UT: Signature Books, 1983–85), 2:276–377.

20  Brigham Young, "Discourse by President Brigham Young, May 18, 1873," *Journal of Discourses* 16:42.

21  C., "My Dear Brother," *Millennial Harbinger* 6, no. 8 (August 1842): 378.

22  Hartwell Ryder, "A Short History of the Foundation of the Mormon Church," 1902. Holograph. Not paginated. Hiram College Library, Hiram, Ohio. Ryder is not always accurate in his chronology of events, and he does not offer evidence supporting his dating of this meeting at the Johnson home. Since a local newspaper reported the same meeting the following month while trying to make a point about the mobbing of Joseph Smith and Sidney Rigdon, it is likely this event happened around the time that Hartwell placed it. The newspaper reported that Joseph declared "that it [personal injury] could not be done—that God would not suffer it; that those who should attempt it, would be miraculously smitten on the spot"; *Geauga Gazette*, April 17, 1832, reprinted as "Triumphs of the Mormon Faith," *Liberal Advocate* 2, no. 10 (April 28, 1832):3. When compared to Nephi's encounter with his brothers in the Book of Mormon, however, it is clear that such declarations only provided temporary protection, since although Nephi's brothers backed down after a similar encounter, a few weeks later they would confront him again and tie him to their ship's mast.

23  Thomas Bullock, Minutes of April Conference, Nauvoo, Illinois, April 6, 1844. General Minutes, CR 100 318, fd. 6. In Richard E. Turley, ed., *Selected Collections from the Archives of the Church of Jesus Christ of Latter-day Saints*, 2 vols. (Provo, UT: BYU Press [December 2002]), DVD, Vol. 1, Disk 18.

24  Robert Charles Brown, *History of Portage County, Ohio*, Chicago: Werner and Beers, 1885, 16½. A description of this event was later published in a series of historical reminiscences in the *Portage County Democrat*, February 15, 1830, 3.

25 Warren Foote, Journal and Autobiography, 1837–1903. MS 12206. Microfilm of typescript. LDS Church History Library. See also Amasa M. Lyman, "Amasa Lyman's History," *Millennial Star* 27, no. 31 (August 5, 1865):487.

26 Staker, *Hearken, O Ye People,* 347.

27 John David Barber, "Statement, 1948," MS 193. Holograph. LDS Church History Library.

28 Staker, *Hearken, O Ye People,* 349.

29 Bullock, Minutes of April Conference, Nauvoo, Illinois, April 6, 1844; capitalization and punctuation added for clarity.

30 Luke Johnson, "History of Luke Johnson," *Millennial Star* 26, no. 12 (December 31, 1864):834–835. B. H. Roberts, ed., *History of the Church* 1:264. Levi W. Hancock, "Autobiography," ca. 1854. MS 5072. Microfilm of holograph. LDS Church History Library, 50.

31 *History of the Church,* 1:262. F. L. Raymond, Letter to J.L. Pitkin, November 6, 1906. LDS Church History Library. George A. Smith, November 15, 1864, *Journal of Discourses,* 11:5, described Warren Waste as directing other mob members.

32 Laura Kimball, "Autobiography of Sister Laura L. Kimball," *Deseret News Weekly* 15 (November 28, 1866):413; Luke Johnson, "History of Luke Johnson," 834–835.

33 *History of the Church,* 1:262.

34 Luke Johnson, "The History of Luke Johnson," 834. Benjamin F. Johnson, Letter to George F. Gibbs 1903. MS 1289. Holograph. LDS Church History Library. Donald Q. Cannon, "Reverend George Moore Comments on Nauvoo, the Mormons, and Joseph Smith," *Western Illinois Regional Studies* 5 (Spring 1982):11. Henry Lewis, *The Valley of the Mississippi Illustrated*, Bertha L. Heilbron, ed. (St. Paul, Minnesota Historical Society, 1967), 248–252. Frederick Kesler in Brian H. Stuy, ed., *Collected Discourses Delivered by President Wilford Woodruff, His Two Counselors, The Twelve Apostles, and Others* (Woodland Hills, UT: B. H. S. Publishing, 1992), 5:35.

35 Dean C. Jessee, Mark Ashurst-McGee, and Richard L. Jensen, eds., *Journals, 1832–1839, The Joseph Smith Papers* (Salt Lake City: The Church Historian's Press, 2008), 1:133.

36 Luke Johnson, "History of Luke Johnson," 835.

37 Heber C. Kimball, Sermon, October 23, 1853, recorded in shorthand by George D. Watt and transcribed by LaJean Carruth, cited in Staker, *Hearken, O Ye People,* 352.

38 Kesler, in Stuy, *Collected Discourses,* 5:35.

39 Staker, *Hearken, O Ye People,* 352–353.

40 Katherine Hulet Winget, "Autobiography," in *Our Pioneer Heritage,* Kate B. Carter, ed. (Salt Lake City: Daughters of the Utah Pioneers, 1970), 13:489.

41 Richard S. Van Wagoner, *Sidney Rigdon: A Portrait of Religious Excess* (Salt Lake City: Signature Books, 1994), 116–118.

42 Staker, *Hearken, O Ye People,* 391–548.

43 Zerah Pulsipher, Autobiographical Sketch, Holograph. LDS Church History Library, 3.

44 Jonathan Dunham, Diaries, Vol. 1, Microfilm of holograph. LDS Church History Library, 16.

# CHAPTER TWO

## MOBBED

## FROM JACKSON COUNTY, MISSOURI, IN 1833

### WILLIAM G. HARTLEY

Settlers watched suspiciously in July 1831 when religious followers of Joseph Smith started to settle in Jackson County, Missouri. These newcomers claimed God wanted that county to be a New Jerusalem, where believers would gather and build a temple and the City of Zion. Jackson County, then only five years old, had a western border beyond which, by federal decree, prairie lands belonged to Native Americans. Locals knew that six months earlier a handful of Mormon missionaries had tried to preach to those tribes until government agents, responding to complaints from ministers, forced them out. County residents who disliked living close to large Indian populations were rankled by the fact that Mormons considered the Native Americans to be Israelites and believed that God wanted Mormons to team up with the Indians to fulfill divine prophecies. In short, locals distrusted these new settlers.

That distrust grew as increasingly more "Mormonites" moved in. Other than the Mormons' affinity for Native Americans, the locals found other issues to fester about. They feared that Joseph Smith's followers would gain control of county offices, disliked the Mormons' communal economic system, believed that Mormons might allow free blacks into their settlements, resented that Mormons believed God wanted them to take over the county even by blood if necessary, and found Mormons' unorthodox religious beliefs way out of step with accepted Christian dogma and practice. It took only two years for the "old settlers" to employ night riders, guns, whips, arson, arrests, thefts, property damage, fear, intimidation, and even murder to rid the county of Mormons by early November 1833.

Jackson County, Missouri, was Zion to the followers of Joseph Smith—the land of their inheritance. However, notwithstanding the promises of the Almighty if they were faithful, the Saints were driven from that land.

Some 1,200 Mormon men, women, and children became their victims; those involved suffered incalculable losses of farmland, homes, household goods, businesses, livestock, crops, health, and loved ones. Forced into exile, they sought support through the courts, from the state of Missouri, and even from the federal government to regain their property or be compensated for it. They received neither. Their sojourn in Jackson County, the "promised land," lasted but twenty-eight months, and once they left, they never could return to build a Zion society there.

## JACKSON COUNTY

Missouri, a part of the Louisiana Purchase, gained statehood in 1820 as part of a compromise that let it into the Union as a slave state. In December 1826, the Missouri legislature authorized the "County of Jackson," named for Tennessee Senator and later United States President Andrew Jackson. The county was initially twenty-seven miles wide and eighty miles long, but in 1833 it shrank by two-thirds when its south section became Van Buren County. Tiny Independence, settled in 1827 near the Missouri River, became the county seat.[1] A two-room cabin became the temporary courthouse.

Jackson County was sparsely populated. The 1830 federal census counted 2,823 residents, including 193 slaves. Land was widely available for as little as $1.25 per acre.[2] Springs percolated water that meandered into the Big Blue and Little Blue rivers, which in turn flowed northward to empty into the Missouri River. The two Blue rivers divided the county into three "townships" east to west: Ft. Osage, Blue, and Kaw. (Saints would settle in Blue and Kaw but not Ft. Osage.) The east-churning Missouri River formed the county's northern border. Throughout the county, except in thick timber patches along streams, fertile

Jackson County was named for United States President Andrew Jackson, a war hero and senator from Tennessee before he became President.

ANDREW JACKSON.

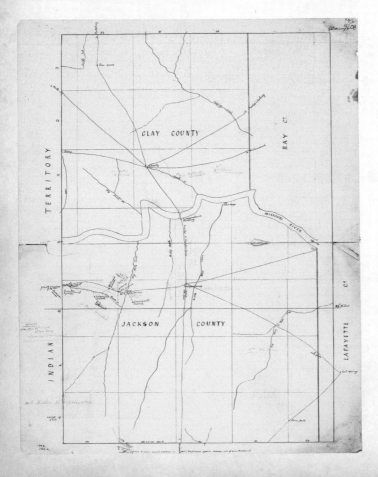

Bottom: Map of Clay and Jackson counties by Thomas Bullock—courtesy of the Church History Library

black prairie soil, three to ten feet deep, produced lush prairie grasses good for stock grazing. Fruits, vegetables, and grains grew readily. Early settlers saw buffalo, elk, turkeys, and geese; ducks were also abundant.[3]

## ZION TO BE BUILT IN JACKSON COUNTY

Six months after Joseph Smith organized the Church of Christ in April 1830 in Fayette, New York, a revelation stated that the City of Zion, the millennial New Jerusalem, was to be built by his followers "on the borders by the Lamanites"
(D&C 28:9). Next, a March 1831 revelation announced that Saints would build a New Jerusalem to be "a city of refuge, a place of safety" (D&C 45:66). Directed by such revelations, Joseph Smith and just fewer than a hundred Saints—twenty-four missionary pairs and members of the Colesville Branch—made a long trip from Ohio to Jackson County in the summer of 1831.

When the Saints first arrived, Independence was a "primitive, busy frontier village," primarily "a collection of log stores, rustic mechanic shops, and scattered brick, log, or clapboard houses."[4] Ezra Booth, among the first Mormons to move there, said Independence in 1831 was "a new town containing a [new] courthouse built of brick, two or three merchant's stores, and 15 or 20 dwelling houses, built mostly of log hewed on both sides."[5]

While Joseph Smith was exploring Jackson County, revelations identified that region as "the land of promise" and specified that Independence was to become "the center place" of Zion, with a site for the temple just west of town (see D&C 57:2–3). Further, "It is wisdom that the land should be purchased by the saints, and also every tract lying westward, even unto the line

D&C 57 was a revelation given to the Prophet Joseph Smith while he was visiting Jackson County in 1831. It designated Independence as the "center place" for Zion.

Opposite Bottom: Independence and Jackson County marked the westernmost border of the United States in 1831 and the beginning of the Oregon and Santa Fe trails. At that time, Independence was a rough frontier town.

Saints enjoyed socializing as they settled Jackson County.

Edward Partridge, a hatter from Painesville, Ohio, joined the Church after meeting the Prophet Joseph Smith in New York. He would be called as the Church's first bishop, ministering to the Saints in Jackson County.

running directly between Jew [Lamanites] and Gentile; And also every tract bordering by the prairies" (D&C 57:4–5). Once obtained, this land would be "an everlasting inheritance" (D&C 57:5). But the revelation also warned that "after much tribulation come the blessings" (D&C 58:4). Such tribulation would strike two years later.

On August 2, 1831, in western Kaw Township, twelve elders ceremoniously laid a log for a meetinghouse as a foundation in Zion, and Sidney Rigdon dedicated this "land of Zion" for the gathering of the Saints. The next day, Joseph Smith and others dedicated the temple site located a half mile west of the brick courthouse in Independence. Before returning to Kirtland, Ohio, he appointed Bishop Edward Partridge to preside over the Missouri settlements and told him to buy lands and promote and receive a systematic gathering of Church members to the county. Joseph Smith assigned Algernon Sidney Gilbert to establish a store, and he instructed Elders William W. Phelps and Oliver Cowdery to start a printing operation. The founding of Zion now was outlined. When Joseph reached Kirtland in late August, he received a revelation urging that "the land of Zion" must be obtained "by purchase or by blood" (see D&C 63:27–30). When Jackson County non-Mormons heard about the "by blood" statement, they primed their rifles.

## MORMON MISFITS

Some Saints who arrived in the summer of 1831, mostly Yankees from the northeast, felt they had stepped down the civilization scale. They found that the earliest settlers included independent-minded Southern farmers, merchants, and mechanics, mostly from Kentucky and Tennessee, joined by a few Santa Fe Trail traders and frequently by the frontier's usual share of suspicious characters—"and an uncultivated, disorderly class drawn by the freedom and frequent lawlessness of the frontier."[6] As a trade depot for western trails, Independence attracted rough types. One minister who visited about 1830 judged the county to be a "godless place," filled with "profane

swearers." Sundays, he said, were days "for merchandising, jollity, drinking, gambling, and general anti-Christian conduct." Men enjoyed gambling on horse races and cockfights. "There are suspicious characters who headquarter here," he observed, who disappeared when lawmen arrived and resurfaced when the coast was clear. Fighting, including eye gouging, was common.[7] One observer said the Christian ministers in that area themselves were "a sad lot of churchmen, untrained, uncouth, given to imbibing spirituous liquors."[8]

Joseph Smith said, after residents had driven the Saints out, that compared to New York and Ohio citizenry, Jackson County settlers exhibited "degradation, leanness of intellect, ferocity and jealousy of a people that were nearly a century behind the times."[9] Newel Knight, leader of the Colesville group of Saints, was not pleased. "Our feelings can be better imagined than described," he said, "when we who had been reared in good society in the East, enjoying the benefits of education and refinement, and who had been surrounded with the comforts and even the luxuries of life," moved into this "semi-barbarian" place.[10] Conversely, locals considered the Mormon newcomers strange and fanatical.

## PIONEERING THE LAND OF ZION, 1831–1833

Bishop Partridge immediately began buying land for the Church and eventually acquired more than two thousand acres in Kaw and Blue townships. Townships are areas six by six miles square containing thirty-six "sections," each one square mile containing 640 acres. Five Mormon settlements developed—four in Kaw Township (Blue River, Whitmer, Colesville, and Prairie Settlements) and one in Blue Township (Independence, which included the temple lot and nearby land). Most Saints lived on Church-owned property, but a few purchased land of their own. "This area was a sacred and dedicated land for the peaceful gathering of the Mormon people," who "anticipated peace and prosperity in their newly found Zion"[11]

Much of Independence was inhabited by Southerners, making the Saints—who were mostly Northerners—unwelcome both because of their faith and their customs.

William W. Phelps was sent to Jackson County by revelation and was charged with the responsibility of printing Church materials.

William W. Phelps—courtesy of the LDS Church Archives

Work brought results. Families built simple shelters; most plowed, planted, and fenced, and their farms produced grain. Most kept livestock. A few planted orchards. Some men and women sought employment wherever they could find it.[12]

Several Mormons engaged in trades and businesses. Sidney Gilbert operated the Gilbert and Whitney store (the bishops' storehouse). William W. Phelps, with the help of Oliver Cowdery and John Whitmer, managed the Church's printing operation; in June 1832, they started publishing the monthly newspaper, the *Evening and Morning Star*. They also published a second newspaper, the *Upper Missouri Advertiser*, and had printed all but the last section of the Book of Commandments when local citizens destroyed the building in July 1833 (see p. 31). Joseph and Newel Knight built and operated a gristmill. Carpenter Levi W. Hancock started a business as a cabinet-maker. Peter Whitmer Jr. did tailoring in an upstairs room rented from Lilburn Boggs, soon to be the state's lieutenant governor.

The Blue River settlement, six miles west of Independence, was possibly the largest Mormon community, with more than three hundred members. There, Porter Rockwell operated the Big Blue River Ferry.

Revelation instructed that those who gathered to Zion should live a new kind of economic order spelled out in "the Law" (see D&C 42).[13] In this Church-supervised cooperative system, the participants agreed to share their property, their labor, and their income.[14] Bishop Partridge received members' consecrations of their properties, and then issued back to them property, based on need, to manage on their own as stewardships. Surpluses "shall be kept in my storehouse, to administer to the poor and needy" (D&C 42:34) and for "purchasing lands" and the "building up of the New Jerusalem" (D&C 42:35).[15] Bishop Partridge implemented the new system but ran into problems, the main one being that too many of the poor and too few of the well-to-do "gathered" to Zion. As a result, there was a short supply of inheritances and surpluses.[16]

Not a trickle, not a flood, but a steady stream of believers flowed into Jackson County, continuing to increase the Mormon population. Saints worked and worshiped together and set up schools, and generally the settlements succeeded and enjoyed peace (see sidebar below). But not all was well in Zion. By January 1833, Joseph Smith felt concerned that their internal bickerings and self-interests made them too "unpure" to keep the promised

D&C 42 was the "Law of the Church" and commanded the Saints to live the law of consecration. This economic order was practiced for a time on the land of Zion in Missouri.

# SAINTS AT PEACE IN JACKSON COUNTY, 1831–1832

They lived in peace and quiet; no lawsuits with each other or with the world; few or no debts were contracted; few promises broken; there were no thieves, robbers, or murderers; few or no idlers; all seemed to worship God with a ready heart. On Sundays the people assembled to preach, pray, sing, and received the ordinances of God. Other days all seemed busy in the various pursuits of industry. In short, there has seldom, if ever, been a happier people upon the earth than the Church of the Saints now were.[59]

*Source: The Autobiography of Parley P. Pratt*

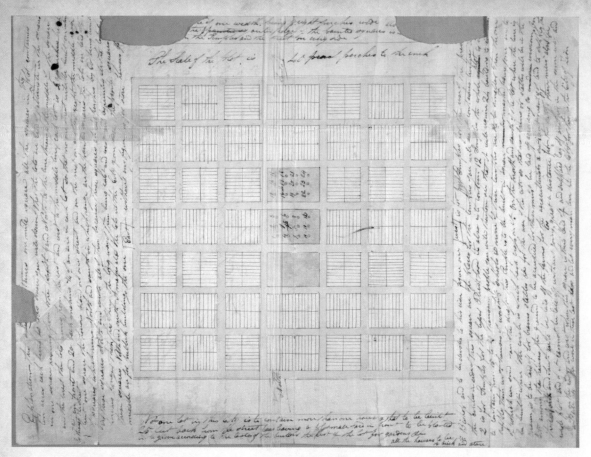

From Kirtland, Ohio, the Prophet Joseph Smith sent plat map drawings laying out the design for the City of Zion to be established in Independence. The plat, later expanded, demonstrated considerable wisdom and insight into city planning and sociality.

land. "If Zion will not purify herself, so as to be approved," he cautioned, God "will seek another people." He warned of "the threatened judgments of God."[17] To purify the flock, Bishop Partridge visited each branch and held "solemn assemblies" for confession and repentance. This effort produced good results.[18]

A festive gathering took place on April 6, 1833, at the Rockwell ferry, where Jackson County Saints celebrated the Church's birthday—the first time any Church group did this. More than five hundred members worshiped and socialized from 10 A.M. until 4 P.M.[19] Then, three months later, the Missouri Saints received a major assignment from Joseph Smith: start building the holy city and temple. In June 1833, he sent drawings and plans, given by revelation, for the City of Zion and for a complex of twenty-four temples. Unfortunately, as the postal service's stagecoaches conveyed that bundle of plans to Missouri, a three-week journey, Jackson County's old settlers went on the warpath to drive out the Mormons.

## JULY 1833 ULTIMATUMS AND ATTACKS

Anti-Mormon gatherings became obvious in April 1833. "We believed them deluded fanatics," upset Jackson County citizenry said. "They declare openly that their God has given them this county of land, and that sooner or later they must and will have the possession of our lands for an inheritance."[20] Mormon numbers reached a thousand or more, or about one-third of the county's population, so civic leaders and rabble decided to physically force them out.[21]

Approximately three hundred upset non-Mormons assembled in Independence, anxious to figure out some way to be rid of the Mormons. "On hearing the news," Newel Knight noted, "the brethren met together and prayed to God to overrule the wicked designs of the mob meeting."[22]

In July, Brother Phelps published an editorial in the *Evening and Morning Star* entitled "Free People of Color," which Missourians misinterpreted to be an invitation for "free Negroes & Mulattoes from other States to become Mormons and remove and settle among us." Enraged local citizens gathered and framed a "Secret Constitution."[23] It proclaimed that "an important crisis is at hand" such that a "company" must be formed to deal with it.

If not constitutional, such a group had the law of nature and of self-preservation on its side. The Mormons were not acceptable, the document asserted, because of their strange religious ideas: conversing face-to-face with God,

The *Evening and Morning Star,* edited by William W. Phelps, was the Church's newspaper in Independence.

receiving direct revelations from heaven, healing the sick by laying on of hands, and performing miracles like those described in the Bible. Particularly disconcerting, a vigilante leader later said, were "these fanatics making boasts that they intended to possess the entire county saying that God had promised it to them and they were going to have it."[24] Eighty citizens signed the "constitution," including the constable, deputy constable, county clerk, postmaster, jailor, an attorney, a judge, three merchants, and two justices of the peace.[25]

Armed with this anti-Mormon document, between four and five hundred Missourians met on July 20 at the Independence courthouse, determined to expel the Mormons peaceably if possible—or "forcibly if we must." They met to adopt methods "to rid themselves of the set of fanatics called Mormons." They approved removals and drafted proposals different from those of the "Secret Constitution"; some newspapers termed their proposals "Propositions of the Mob."[26] The proposals were peppered with anti-Mormon claims—that Mormons were becoming too numerous, that new arrivals were of the poorer classes, that Mormons talked of taking control of the county "by the sword," and particularly that Mormons were encouraging free blacks in other states to join their communities. "It requires no gift of prophecy to tell that the day is not far distant, when the government of the county will be in their hands, or persons willing to court their favor from motives of interest or ambition." They maintained that such must not happen:

> What would be the fate of our lives and prop-
> erty in the hands of jurors and witnesses who do not
> blush to declare, and would not upon occasion hesi-
> tate, to swear that they have wrought miracles and
> supernatural cures; have conversed with God and his
> angels, and possess and exercise the gift of divination
> and of unknown tongues, and fired with the prospect
> of obtaining inheritances without money and with-
> out prices, may be better imagined than described.[27]

Of utmost concern, they did not want the disreputable Mormons controlling county offices and civic affairs. "Fear of religious aliens in power," historian Richard Bushman found, "lay at the heart of gentile hatreds and fears."[28] The assemblage approved resolutions that required that (1) no new Mormons should move into the county; (2) those in the county must pledge to leave within a reasonable time; (3) the Saints' newspaper must cease publishing immediately; (4) Mormon leaders must make the above actions happen; and (5) those who fail to comply will suffer consequences.

A committee carried these ultimatums to Mormon elders and ordered them to pledge "full and complete" compliance. Put on the spot, William W. Phelps, Edward Partridge, Algernon Sidney Gilbert, John Corrill, John Whitmer, and Isaac Morley asked for three months to deliberate. They were told no. Ten days? Again, no. How much time? Fifteen minutes. The elders said no, ending the negotiations.[29]

Shocked by the Mormons' refusal, citizens took action. About a hundred people vandalized the two-story *Evening and Morning Star* office. They tossed the printing press, the type, printed materials (including the almost fully typeset Book of Commandments pages), and furniture outside, scattering them. Then they pulled off the roof and knocked down the walls. Vandals broke into the Gilbert and Whitney store and tossed bolts of cloth and other goods into the street. They raided a blacksmith shop and threw tools into the street. While despoiling spread, some Missourians forced Bishop Partridge and Charles Allen to the public square, partially stripped them, and, amid swearing and cheering by a lively crowd, brutally tarred and feathered their prisoners. Citizens beat one Mormon with thongs and hickory branches.[30]

On July 20, 1833, an angry mob destroyed the Church-owned press of the *Evening and Morning Star* and tossed the unfinished Book of Commandments into the street.

Bishop Edward Partridge was taken out onto the public square in Independence and threatened with a demand to denounce his religion. Bishop Partridge refused to deny the faith and was tarred and feathered.

The vigilante mob disbanded but then reassembled on July 23. Between three and five hundred men, "some armed with fire arms, dirks, and sticks, with their red flags hoisted," entered Independence.[31] Part of them rounded up Mormon leaders and assembled them on the public square. The elders—under threats that men, women, and children would be beaten with whips, houses demolished, and fields burned— signed an agreement that the Saints would leave the county: half by January 1, 1834, and the rest by April. The mob accepted this coerced pledge and promised no further violence if the Mormons carried it out. Nevertheless, anti-Mormon abuses continued.[32]

## NO INTENTION TO LEAVE

Fearful, angry Saints resumed their normal activities. They did not expect to honor the pledge because they intended to obey God and establish the City of Zion and the temple. "I continued labor upon a gristmill I was building," Newel Knight said, while "many finished off their houses and went to preparing for the future development of Zion."[33]

In September, eight men in the Colesville Branch signed subscriptions ranging from $20 to $100 in grain or labor to help pay for the temple.[34] Also in September, leaders increased the number of branches from five to ten, each with a high priest in charge. Among the new branch presidents were David Whitmer, Thomas B. Marsh, and Parley P. Pratt.[35]

# DESTRUCTION, SHOOTINGS, AND BLOODSHED

Because Church leaders had signed the agreement to vacate the county under duress, they appealed to Missouri Governor Daniel Dunklin, asking that the state protect them and their property. In response, Governor Dunklin urged the Saints to seek resolution through the courts. Saints then hired a team of lawyers. Feeling they had the governor's support, the leaders announced on October 20 their intention to stay and to defend themselves while pursuing court action. That act of defiance unleashed the war dogs.

Eleven days later, on October 31, the old settlers and "many rowdies" attacked the Mormon settlements on the Big Blue. They unroofed ten houses, beat several unarmed men with sticks and guns, and pelted others with rocks. On October 31 and November 1, "there was one continual scene of outrages of the most hideous kind."[36] An attack came on November 1 designed to destroy the Knight grist mill in the Colesville settlement. Parley P. Pratt and about sixty men, despite rains, posted themselves as guards. Joseph Knight Jr. noted that "many gathered around my mill to save it."[37] That night Pratt caught two Missouri spies. They struck him, cutting his head. His shouts attracted guards, who captured the two. By having hostages, Pratt said, they prevented raiders from attacking. In the morning the two prisoners were given their guns and were released.[38]

That same night, bands of ten to twenty marauders attacked Mormon homes in Independence. They broke into the Gilbert and Whitney store about midnight, scattering "calicoes, handkerchiefs, shawls, and cambricks" into the streets. The next morning all the Mormon families in Independence moved with their belongings to the temple lot—a half mile from the public square—for safety, where about thirty Mormon guards protected them. A boy in that protected group later recalled: "Finally the women and household goods of the members of the Church were taken . . . and piled up there on the Temple Plot in the woods, and we were there, I think it was three days. . . . They were yelling and hollering and swearing and shooting around there night and day."[39]

In 1833, the Saints petitioned Daniel Dunklin, the governor of Missouri, for relief from mob oppression. In return, Governor Dunklin told the Saints to seek help from the courts, but when the mobs learned of the Saints' efforts to fight back, their wrath intensified.

The mobs showed no pity, even for the weak. The Saints were driven out of Jackson County, seeking shelter and refuge wherever they could find it. The records witness that their flight out of the county was marked with bloody footprints in the snow.

The violence peaked on November 4 at the "Battle above the Blue." On November 2, mob members painted like Indians struck the Big Blue settlement. They took over the Rockwell ferry on the Big Blue, destroyed property, and harassed nearby Saints. They tore down several log buildings and beat and shot David Bennett, leaving him for dead. David Whitmer marched fifteen volunteers to the rescue, but marauders came after them and tried to hunt them down, searching corn fields and houses. Learning of this, Colesville Branch Saints sent about thirty men with fifteen guns and pitchforks to reinforce their friends. The rescuers reached Christian Whitmer's house at sunset, where mob members were bullying him. They surprised the mob, whose members opened fire. Mormons shot back, causing the ruffians to flee.

The brief skirmish left two mob members and Mormon Andrew Barber dead; in addition, several on both sides were injured. Among the Mormons, William Whiting's foot was shot and mangled. Henry Cleveland was shot in the right shoulder. Jacob Whitmer was shot in his right wrist.[40] Brother Philo Dibble was shot in the stomach. An experienced doctor checked him and declared the wounds fatal. Eluding a mob near the house where Dibble lay, Newel Knight slipped inside, went to the victim's bed, and blessed him. Dibble experienced a miraculous healing (see the sidebar on p. 36). For ten successive days with only three or four men to aid them, some 120 women and children concealed themselves in the woods in fear of being massacred.[41]

On November 5, hearing that a half dozen Mormons had been imprisoned in Independence, Lyman Wight led about a hundred Mormon defenders from Kaw Township settlements to the rescue. "A report reached Independence," a witness said, "that the Mormons were marching in a body towards the town, with the intention of sacking and burning it. I had often heard the cry of 'Indians!' announcing the approach of hostile savages, but I do not remember ever to have witnessed so much consternation as prevailed at Independence on this memorable occasion."[42]

*Out of Independence by Jim Larson*

News of bloodshed at the "Battle above the Blue" generated calls for revenge among the "old citizens." To stop open warfare, Lieutenant Governor Lilburn W. Boggs called out the Missouri militia, which included mob leaders. Commanded by an active anti-Mormon, it disarmed the Saints, making it impossible for them to defend themselves. After November 6, armed and mounted Missourians raided the Mormon settlements. Companies of fifty to eighty men broke into Mormon houses, searched for weapons, whipped men, and fired shots. "Thus we were obliged, not only by the *mob*, but also by the *militia* to leave the county," John Corrill wrote.[43]

During this war against the Saints, which extended from July to November and beyond, citizens and criminal types raided Mormon settlements; tore down and burned cabins; destroyed fences; stole furniture, tools, equipment, and livestock; killed pigs, chickens, and cows; burned haystacks and crops; trampled gardens; terrified and threatened men, women, and children; and shot at, horse-whipped, and beat up Mormon men, injuring a score or more. Mormons lost an enormous amount of property—but more than that, as their petitions for redress later lamented, they were deprived of their citizenship and their civil rights. One of the mob members years later felt no hesitation to say that "there was no pretense of legality in any of the proceedings, only a unanimous determination to drive out the Mormons . . . Or be themselves driven out."[44]

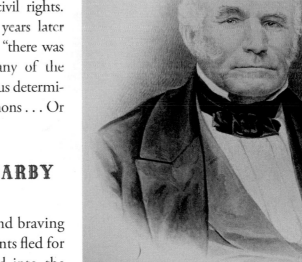

## ESCAPES INTO NEARBY COUNTIES

Fearing for their lives and braving cold November weather, Saints fled for safety to others' homes and into the woods. Small groups tried to reach the Missouri River ferries. Joseph Knight Jr. witnessed women and children walking all hours of the night, with bare feet on the frozen ground, crying because of the cold. He continued to mill grain so that Saints could take flour with them.[45]

It was Lieutenant Governor Lilburn W. Boggs who called out the Missouri State Militia to quell the violence in Jackson County. The militia would disarm the Mormon defenders, leading to their expulsion from the state.

Finding various escape routes, the Saints became scattered. Refugee clusters fled south into Van Buren County, crossing prairie that had recently been burned to charred, sharp stubble.

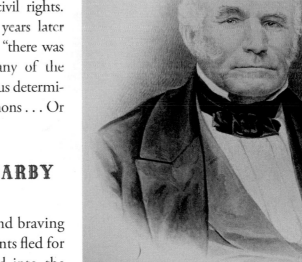

# PHILO DIBBLE'S
# MIRACULOUS HEALING

During attacks that drove the Saints from Jackson County in October–November 1833, Philo Dibble was shot in the stomach. An experienced doctor checked him and declared the wounds would be fatal. Eluding a mob near the house where Dibble lay, Newel Knight slipped inside and went to the victim's bed. "I drew the bed curtains with one hand and laid the other upon his head, praying secretly" in his behalf, Newel said. Then he left immediately to avoid the mob. The next day, business took Newel some ten miles from the place, where, to his surprise, "I met Bro. Dibble making his escape from the county":

He told me that as soon as I placed my hand on his head the pain and sore-ness seemed gradually to move as before a power driving it, until in a few minutes it left his body. He then discharged about a gallon of putrid matter, and the balls and pieces of clothing which had passed into his body.

Philo Dibble also wrote about this wonderful healing, and his account adds details not in Newel Knight's recounting:

After the surgeon left me, Brother Newell Knight came to see me. He sat on the right side of my bed and laid his hand on my head but never spoke. I felt the Spirit resting upon me at the crown of my head before his hand touched me, and I knew immediately that I was going to be healed. It seemed to form like a ring under the skin and followed down my body. When the ring came to the wound, another ring formed around the first bullet hole, also the second and third. Then the ring formed on each shoulder and on each hip and followed down to my fingers and toes and left me.

I immediately arose and discharged three quarts of blood or more, with some pieces of my clothes that had been driven into my body by the bullets. I then dressed myself and went out doors. . . . From that time not a drop of blood came from me and I never afterwards felt the slightest pain or inconvenience from my wound except that I was somewhat weak from the loss of blood.[60]

"O how did our hearts rejoice and give thanks to God," Newel wrote, "who had heard and answered the petitions although offered up secretly in behalf of this servant while surrounded with fiends in human form." Brother Dibble lived for many years.

*Source:* William G. Hartley, *Stand by My Servant Joseph: The Story of the Joseph Knight Family and the Restoration* (Salt Lake City, UT: Deseret Book, 2003), 176–177. *Source: The Autobiography of Parley P. Pratt.*

# SPECTACULAR METEOR SHOWER

Shortly after midnight, in the morning of November 13, the Mormons encamped along the river bottoms saw the heavens "enveloped in splendid fireworks" and "thousands of bright meteors" shoot in every direction, "with long trains of light following in their course."[1] This Leonid meteor shower lasted several hours, from about 1:00 or 2:00 A.M. until daybreak. It was a spectacle few who saw it ever forgot. The meteors showered down as thick as snowflakes and were like a show of stars dancing about in every direction with the speed of lightning. People went from tent to tent, waking up sleeping Saints to see the heavenly show. Even Joseph Smith and Kirtland Saints saw the display that same early morning. It was seen from the Rocky Mountains to New York City. Some Saints saw it as a sign that God would soon open the way for them to return to Jackson County, others that Christ's Second Coming was near at hand.[2]

Astronomers have determined that the Leonids shower happens every year around mid-November, but rarely is notable, averaging perhaps fifteen bright meteors per hour. But, the Leonids "go wild" every thirty-three years or so. The 1833 shower changed science. Estimates are 50,000 meteors fell per hour, so many scientists finally had to admit that meteors were rocks from the sky. (The Leonids' most spectacular display on record came in 1966, showering some 144,000 meteors an hour. Witnesses said the sky seemed to be "raining stars.")[3]

1   Pratt, *Autobiography*, 97, 103.

2   Several descriptions of the meteor shower by the home-less Saints are in Max H. Parkin, "Latter-day Saints in Clay County," 44–47. For Kirtland observations, including Joseph Smith's, see *History of the Church* 1:439–440.

3   "Night of 'Raining Stars' Expected in '98 or '99," *Deseret News*, Dec. 21, 1996.

# MORMON REFUGEE CAMPS ON MISSOURI RIVER BOTTOMS, NOVEMBER 7, 1833

[The Missouri River] began to be lined on both sides of the ferry with men, women and children; goods, wagons, boxes, provisions, etc., while the ferry was constantly employed; and when night again closed upon us the cottonwood bottom had much the appearance of a camp meeting. Hundreds of people were seen in every direction, some in tents and some in the open air around the fires, while the rain descended in torrents. Husbands were inquiring for their wives, wives for their husbands; parents for their children, and children for their parents. Some had the good fortune to escape with their families, household goods, and some provisional goods. The scene was indescribable.

*Source: Autobiography of Parley P. Pratt*

Children's bare feet became so cut and worn that it was easy to track them by the blood left on the earth. Most Saints sought refuge to the north in Clay County, crossing the Missouri River using a dozen ferries, rowboats, or other craft in which locals rowed them across. Ferries, propelled by oars or sweeps, sometimes required a half day to make a round trip. In present-day dollars it cost nearly $40 to ferry a loaded wagon and team. Within days Mormon refugee camps lined the Missouri River bottoms on the Clay County side (see sidebar at left).

## DRIVING THE LAST SAINTS OUT

Prairie Settlement was the farthest west Mormon branch, located about twelve miles west of Independence on 516 acres purchased by Bishop Partridge. Residents of Prairie Settlement felt safe until November 24, when they too were attacked. Riders chased branch president Lyman Wight for five or six miles across open prairie. Having the faster horse he escaped, and then "lay three weeks in the woods, and was three days and nights without food." About 150 Prairie Settlement Saints went south into Van Buren County, but a few built shelters in southern Jackson County. This infuriated some of the anti-Mormons in Jackson County, who rushed them in January 1834, burned their scanty cabins, and scattered the occupants.[46] That action completed the removal of Mormons from Jackson County.

## THE VICTIMS AND THEIR LOSSES

A memorial penned nine years later as part of the Saints' efforts to be compensated for their Missouri losses summarized the damages done:[47] "Their abandoned houses numbering about 200 were burned down or otherwise demolished by the mob, who destroyed at the same time much of their crops, furniture, and stock. The damage done to the property of the Saints, by the mob . . . as near as they can ascertain would amount to the sum of one hundred and twenty thousand dollars."

Scores of petitioners for redress recounted their sufferings and losses. Benjamin Slade, for example, had to leave ten acres of improvement, a house, stable, corn crib, six acres of wheat on the ground, two stacks of wheat, one stack of rye, two stacks of oats, five or six tons of hay, thirty to forty barrels of corn, fifty or sixty bushels of potatoes, a hundred bushels of turnips, two horses, seven head of young cattle, six hogs, fowls, and furniture. He estimated his total losses at $1,000.[48] Ormond Butler had his house burned, corn and other crops destroyed, and cows taken by the mob.[49] Titus Billings testified that the mob burned his twenty-four tons of hay "to ashes," burned down his house and barn, and destroyed his four acres of wheat.[50] John Loveless said a mob "told me to leave my house forth with or they would shoot me & my family in the house & burn all together." When he and his family left with only what they could carry on their backs, the mob shot at him, "the ball grazing my face so as to Draw Blood." Loveless said that "I saw them shoot down several hogs and cattle and left them lying."[51]

A mob of about fifty men captured Truman Brace. One assailant beat him with an axe handle; after about fifty strokes it broke, so he used rawhide to whip Brace. Another man struck

The Lord, by revelation, commanded the Saints to petition the government for redress for their losses.

Brace's head with a rifle. Inside Brace's house they sat him on a chair; a man thrust the muzzle of a gun against his neck, pushed him against the wall, and kicked him on the mouth with his foot, cutting Brace's lip. The mob then took a friend of Brace's outside and whipped him. They plundered Brace's house and property. When unable to cross the Missouri for safety, he fled southward and left his crops for the mob. In his flight he found some eight or ten children wandering the frozen prairie "with bare feet much bloody." He suffered such cold and fatigue that he "wished for death."[52] (See sidebar right for other accounts.)

## NO RETURN TO JACKSON COUNTY OR COMPENSATIONS

On December 12, 1833, Parley Pratt, Newel Knight, and John Corrill published a circular that documented and detailed the anti-Mormons' crimes in Jackson County. Hoping to influence public opinion, elders sent that circular to newspapers, circulated it locally, and sent a copy to United States President Andrew Jackson. Probably penned primarily by Parley P. Pratt, the document showed that "the destruction of crops, household furniture, and clothing, is very great; and much of their stock is lost."[53]

In June 1834, the Prophet Joseph, grieved by the expulsion and confident that Missouri's governor would help the Saints return if he had enough military force, arrived from Ohio with a small army called Zion's Camp. Saints and Missourians wondered if the Mormon army would invade Jackson County and win back the lost property. But it quickly became clear that Governor Daniel Dunklin would provide no military resources to help the Saints return home (see sidebar on p. 42). On June 22, while Zion's Camp was encamped near Jackson County, Joseph Smith received a revelation (see D&C 105) in which the Lord charted a non-war course for Missouri Saints. And, rather than criticize the Jackson County aggressors, it chastised Saints for not aiding the poor and not doing more to build up Zion in Jackson County. Therefore, "mine elders should wait for a little season for the redemption of Zion" (D&C 105:9) and be chastened "until they learn obedience" (D&C 105:6).

The displaced Saints were admonished to "make proposals for peace unto those who have smitten you" (D&C 105:40). So twelve of the leading elders authored "An Appeal" and published it that August. It was designed to calm Missouri fears fanned hot by the Zion's Camp army. It appealed for peace. It spelled

# SAMPLE ACCOUNTS OF VICTIMS' LOSSES IN JACKSON COUNTY

## SOLOMON CHAMBERLAIN

1833. I was driven from Jackson Co MO with the loss of my inheritance and left my crops on the ground two houses burned and the loss of some cattle I was there between 2 and 3 years and the loss that I sustained I should Say was not less than $2,000.00.

## THOMAS CRANDALL

7½ acres of corn $70.00

36 bushels potatoes 18.00

2 cows 30.00

6 calves 18.00

12 hogs 25.00

## LYDIA B. ENGLISH

Expense moving to Missouri $130

Loss Jackson Co house and chair

Shop, land & garden vegetables $1,500

My husband Wm Whiting being wounded by the Mob in Jackson Co the exposures & hardships were too much for his feeble constitution to bear he died in Oct following the pain & distress of his body as well as mind, likewise the distress of my family all sick at once the hardships & privations caused by such a violation of the laws of the Land, the disstress of mind, driven from home in the chily month of Nov to seek a home among strangers, no money can amply atone for such losses & crosses $5,000.

## ALVIN C. GRAVES

To being driven from Jackson County being forced to leave my land of two hundred and forty acres with a good improvement of a house and about 340 acres under fence and tanyard with about one thousand dollars worth of stock ordered off by a mob headed by Gabrael Fitzhugh and the loss of my crop, $5,000.00

## PHILO JUDD

Fired on by mob without cause or provocation, killed one man with him, wounded several others, mob forced him out "Names of some of said mob Hugh L Barzeal, James Campbell, James McGee, and others too numerous to mention."

## JOSEPH KNIGHT JR.

Expense of moving $25

a mill burned down 200

a house burned 50

3 acres of land and 50 peach trees 50

hay and corn 25

Source: Clark V. Johnson, ed., *Mormon Redress Petitions: Documents of the 1833–1838 Missouri Conflict* (Provo, UT: BYU Religious Studies Center, 1992), 159, 173–174, 197, 219, 254, 259.

# MISSOURI GOVERNOR DANIEL DUNKLIN'S DISTASTE FOR "THE POOR DELUDED MORMONS"

Missouri Governor Daniel Dunklin wanted nothing to do with assisting the Saints to get back into Jackson County, as shown by his comments in an August 15, 1834, letter to Joel H. Haden:

Upon the subject of the poor deluded Mormons & the infuriated Jacksonites, it is unnecessary now to say anything & I hope it will continue so. There can be no difficulty in ascertaining the correct course for me to pursue if I am compelled to act. I have no regard for the Mormons, as a separate people; & have an utter contempt for them as a religious sect; while on the other hand I have much regard for the people of Jackson county, both personally and politically; they are, many of them, my personal friends, and nearly all of them are very staunch democrats; but these are secondary considerations when my duties are brought into question.

*Source:* Daniel Dunklin to Joel H. Haden, August 15, 1834, in the Daniel Dunklin Papers at the Missouri State Historical Society, Columbus, MO.

out grievances the Saints carried. It explained that the Saints could not accept a Jackson County committee's proposal to "buy or sell" because "to sell our land would amount to a denial of our faith, as that land is the place where the Zion of God shall stand." That's not all: Mormons could not buy all the county because of exorbitant prices being asked and other unreasonable requirements. The "Appeal" that Saints be allowed to return to Jackson County and be compensated for stolen or burned property fell on deaf ears. For years it was unsafe even for individual Saints to return to Jackson County to reclaim property or conduct business.

On May 26, 1835, a Church council in Kirtland assigned inheritances in Jackson County to forty-nine men, if and when Saints could go back, including six Colesville Branch members.[54] But dreams of returning to Jackson County never materialized. Between 1839 and 1842, Saints at Joseph Smith's request prepared affidavits to secure redress from the federal government for losses suffered in Missouri. Scores of claims listed Jackson County losses.[55] None received compensation. An 1841 revelation decreed that because Saints had "been hindered by the hands of their enemies, and by oppression" from returning to Jackson County, they were now freed from that obligation (see D&C 124:49–54). In time, Church agents went to Jackson County to sell or trade Mormon lands to raise money for Church needs elsewhere.[56] Bishop Partridge died in 1840, and in 1848 his heirs sold their claim to the temple lot's sixty-three acres for $300, as advised by Brigham Young.[57] In 1907, the LDS Church officially returned to Independence and set up a mission headquarters there.[58]

* * *

The brutal story of the expulsion of the Mormons from Jackson County was, by any measure, a crime and a tragedy. It proved to be the first of several such mistreatments and miscarriages of justice that victimized Church members during the nineteenth century. But it was just a county-level civil war against the Saints. By comparison, subsequent campaigns escalated to the state level, and ultimately prosecutions and persecutions came at the hand of the federal government.

Joseph Smith received what would later become D&C 105 near the end of the Zion's Camp march. In this revelation the Lord taught "my people must needs be chastened until they learn obedience." He also commanded that "mine elders should wait for a little season for the redemption of Zion."

# Endnotes

1    Ezra Booth description, July 1831, cited in Ronald E. Romig, *Early Independence, Missouri: "Mormon" History Tour Guide* (Independence, MO: Missouri Mormon Frontier Foundation, 1994), 13.

2    Warren Abner Jennings, *Zion Is Fled: The Expulsion of the Mormons from Jackson County, Missouri*, Ph.D. dissertation, University of Florida, 1961, 13, 17.

3    Max H. Parkin and LaMar C. Berrett, *Sacred Places, Vol. 4: Missouri: A Comprehensive Guide to Early LDS Historical Sites* (Salt Lake City: Deseret Book, 2004), 8; William W. Phelps's letter to Oliver Cowdery, Oct. 20, 1834, published in [Kirtland, OH] *Messenger and Advocate* (November 1834), 22–23.

4    Parkin and Berrett, 12.

5    Booth's description is quoted in Max H. Parkin, "The Courthouse Mentioned in the Revelation on Zion," *BYU Studies* 14 (Summer 1974), 456.

6    Parkin and Berrett, 8.

7    Ronald E. Romig, *Early Jackson County, Missouri: The "Mormon Settlement" on the Big Blue Rivers* (Independence, MO: Missouri Mormon Trails Foundation, 1996), v–vi.

8    Quoted in Richard L. Bushman, *Joseph Smith: Rough Stone Rolling* (New York: Alfred A. Knopf, 2005), 162.

9    Romig, *Early Jackson County*, v–vi.

10   Newel Knight Journal, Allen Version, LDS Church History Library, Salt Lake City, UT.

11   Parkin and Berrett, 4.

12   Austin, Emily [Coburn Slate], *Mormonism: Or, Life among the Mormons* (Madison, WI: Cantwell Book and Job Printer, 1882), 66.

13   See also D&C 51.

14   Leonard J. Arrington, Feramorz Y. Fox, and Dean L. May, *Building the City of God* (Salt Lake City: Deseret Book, 1976), 15–21.

15   Arrington, Fox, and May, *Building the City of God*, 15.

16   Arrington, Fox, and May, *Building the City of God*, 15–40; Lyndon W. Cook, *Joseph Smith and the Law of Consecration* (Provo, UT: Grandin Book Company, l985), 1–38. Regarding consecration efforts in Missouri, see Jennings, *Zion Is Fled*, Chapter 3, and Porter's "The Colesville Branch in Kaw Township," in *Regional Studies in Latter-day Saint Church History: Missouri*, Arnold K. Garr and Clark V. Johnson, eds. (Provo, UT: BYU Department of Church History and Doctrine, 1994), 280–284.

17   Joseph Smith, *History of the Church of Jesus Christ of Latter-day Saints*, B. H. Roberts, ed. (Salt Lake City: Deseret Book, 1965), 1:316.

18   Donald Q. Cannon and Lyndon W. Cook, eds., *Far West Record: Minutes of the Church of Jesus Christ of Latter-day Saints, 1830–1844* (Salt Lake City: Deseret Book, 1983); see footnote on p. 61.

19   *Evening and Morning Star*, April 1833, 5.

20   From Missourian's "Secret Constitution," which Joseph Smith dubbed the "Manifesto of the Mob" (*History of the Church* 1:374–377). Quotes are on p. 375. The entire document is quoted with no title in Jennings, *Zion Is Fled*, 136–137.

21   General history about anti-Mormon violence in Jackson County is drawn from Jennings, *Zion Is Fled*; Jennings, "The Expulsion of the Mormons from Jackson County, Missouri," *Missouri Historical Review* 64 (October 1969), 41–63; *History of the Church, I*; and Parley Pratt, Newel Knight, and John Corrill, "'The Mormons' So Called," in the *Evening and Morning Star, Extra,* February 1834, reprinted in *BYU Studies* 14 (Summer 1974), 505–515.

22   William G. Hartley, *Stand by My Servant Joseph: The Story of the Joseph Knight Family and the Restoration* (Salt Lake City: Deseret Book, 2003), 164.

23   Full document cited in Jennings, *Zion Is Fled*, 135–137; quote is on p. 137.

24   Colonel Thomas L. Pitcher, in *Kansas City Journal*, June 19, 1881, cited in Parkin and Berrett, 114.

25   Jennings, *Zion Is Fled*, 134–135.

26   The full "Propositions of the Mob" document is found in *History of the Church* 1:396–398.

27   *History of the Church* 1:397.

28   Richard L. Bushman, "Mormon Persecutions in Missouri," *BYU Studies* 3 (Autumn 1960), 20.

29   Jennings, *Zion Is Fled*, 142–143.

30   Jennings, *Zion Is Fled*, 143–147.

31   The description of July 23 mobs with red flags is from the account by Knight, Pratt, and Corrill, Feb. 1834.

32   Jennings, *Zion Is Fled*, 148–156.

33   Newel Knight Journal, Folder 1, unpaginated, Church History Library.

34   Hartley, *Stand by My Servant Joseph*, 170–172.

35   *Far West Record*, 65–66, Sept. 11, 1833.

36   The *Evening and Morning Star, Extra*, February 1834.

37   Joseph Knight Jr., "Incidents of History," Holograph, LDS Church History Library, Salt Lake City, Utah, 3.

38  Newel Knight's Journal, *Scraps of Biography: Tenth Book of the Faith-Promoting Series* (Salt Lake City: Juvenile Instructor's Office, 1883, reprinted in Salt Lake City by Bookcraft, 1969), 81; and Pratt, *Autobiography*, 97.

39  Jennings, *The Expulsion of the Mormons*, 13.

40  Smith, *History of the Church* 1:431; Parkin and Berrett, 102.

41  Johnson, *Petitions*, 398.

42  Josiah Gregg, *The Commerce of the Prairie*, 1844, Milo M. Quaife, ed., and reprinted in 1967 by Bison Books (Lincoln, NE).

43  An excellent account of the Oct. 31 to Nov. 7 events is John Corrill's December 1833 letter to Oliver Cowdery, published in the *Evening and Morning Star* (Kirtland), Jan. 1834.

44  John C. McCoy in 1885, quoted in Parkin and Berrett, 92–93.

45  Joseph Knight Jr., "Incidents of History," 3.

46  Parkin and Berrett, 119–120.

47  "The Second Memorial," to the Senate and House of Representatives, Jan. 10, 1842, signatures Elias Higbee, John Taylor, Elias Smith, in Johnson, *Petitions*, 398.

48  Johnson, *Petitions*, 535.

49  Johnson, *Petitions*, 150.

50  Johnson, *Petitions*, 138–140.

51  Johnson, *Petitions*, 279, 491.

52  Johnson, *Petitions*, 144, 421.

53  Pratt, Knight, and Corrill, Feb. 1834, 505–515.

54  Richard L. Anderson and Scott H. Faulring, eds., "The Documentary History of Oliver Cowdery, Preliminary Draft," in author's possession, Vol. 3:118. The Colesville men assigned inheritances were Father Joseph Knight, Newel and Joseph Knight Jr., Hezekiah and Ezekiel Peck, and Freeborn DeMille.

55  Johnson, *Petitions*. See "Jackson County" in the index.

56  Parkin and Berrett, 12.

57  Parkin and Berrett, 27.

58  Parkin and Berrett, 17.

59  Parley P. Pratt Jr., ed., *Autobiography of Parley P. Pratt* (Salt Lake City: Deseret Book, 1985), 93.

60  Hartley, *Stand by My Servant Joseph*, 175–177.

Head Quarters of the Militia
City of Jefferson

Octr 27 1838

Sir

Since the order of this morning to you
directing you to raise 400 mounted men to be
raised within your division I have received by
Amos Reas Esqr of Ray & Wily C Williams
one of my Aids information of the most appal
-ling Character which entirely changes the face
of things and places the Mormons in the attitude
of an open and avowed defiance of the laws
And of having Made war upon the people of
this State Your orders are therefore to hasten your
operations with all possible speed The Mormons
Must be treated as enemies and must be ex-
-terminated or driven from the State if necessary
for the public peace their outrages are beyond
all description If you can increase your force
you are Authorized to do so to any extent you
may consider necessary I have just issued
orders to Majr Genl Willock of Marion Co to
raise 500 men and to March them to the
Northern part of Davies and there unite with
Genl Doniphon of Clay who has been ordered
with 500 men to procede to the same point for
the purpose of intercepting the retreat of the
Mormons to the North they have been directed
to Communicate with you by express, you Can
also communicate with them if you find it ne
cessary Instead therefore of proceeding as at
first directed to reinstate the Citizens of Davis
in their homes you will procede immediately
to Rickmond and there operate against the
Mormons Brig Genl Parks of Ray has been
ordered to have four hundred of his Brigade

# CHAPTER THREE

# WAR OF EXTERMINATION

## The 1838 Mormon Conflict in Northern Missouri

ALEXANDER L. BAUGH

One of the most infamous names in early Mormon history is that of Missouri Governor Lilburn W. Boggs (1796–1860). His notoriety among Latter-day Saints is due primarily to an executive directive he issued on October 27, 1838, known as the "Extermination Order," which declared that "the Mormons must be treated as enemies and must be exterminated or driven from the State if necessary for the public peace."[1] Within three days, a state militia composed of 2,500 troops was situated on the outskirts of the Mormon settlement of Far West, calling for the surrender of the Mormons and demanding they comply with the governor's mandate. Faced with no alternative, approximately six thousand Latter-day Saints left the state and found refuge and sanctuary in Illinois.

The action taken by Governor Boggs raises several questions. Why did he issue the order? What did he mean that the Mormons "must be exterminated or driven from the State if necessary"? What were his intentions? Did the order authorize full-scale annihilation, or was it one of removal? And finally, what events led him to take such action? The answers to these questions lie in the events associated with the 1838 Mormon-Missouri War—the only state-authorized and state-sanctioned military conflict ever engaged against a religious minority population in the history of the United States.

## BACKGROUND TO THE 1838 MORMON-MISSOURI CONFLICT

Following the expulsion of the Mormons from Jackson County in late 1833, most of the exiles sought refuge in Clay County. Here they found the local citizenry to be more open and tolerant than Jackson's old-time settlers, many of whom offered lodging and employment. During the next two years (1834–1836), the

Upon hearing the distorted reports about the battle at Crooked River, Governor Lilburn W. Boggs became convinced that the Mormons were in a state of rebellion and issued his order of extermination.

MAP BY JOHN HAMER

Within the map:
Area Enlarged
MISSOURI
(attached to Daviess)
(attached to Livingston)
(attached to Linn)
DAVIESS
LINN
Adam-ondi-Ahman
Gallatin • Millport
Grand River
Chillicothe
(attached to Clinton)
Shoal Creek
Hawn's Mill
Far West
LIVINGSTON
CLINTON
CALDWELL
Grand River
CHARITON
Tinney's Grove
BUNCOMBE STRIP
(attached to Ray)
To Chariton
CARROLL
Little
Fishing
River
Crooked River
DeWitt
CLAY
Carrollton
Fishing River
RAY
Richmond
Missouri River
McIlwaine's
Bend
Liberty
Lexington
SALINE
Independence
LAFAYETTE
JACKSON
CASS
JOHNSON
PETTIS

miles
0    5    10
0    10    20
kilometers

After the Latter-day Saints were driven from Jackson County in 1833, many of them took refuge in Clay County, Missouri. Though the residents of Clay County initially welcomed them, it was meant only to be a temporary accommodation.

Mormons purchased land and established more than a dozen small scattered settlements, most of them situated south of Liberty, the county seat. Mormon immigration to the region also continued, though not as extensively as during the Jackson period.

By 1836, approximately 1,500 Latter-day Saints resided in Clay County. However, Clay's citizens never anticipated nor intended that the Latter-day Saints would remain in the county permanently. With a growing Mormon presence in the county, increased tensions and threats of hostilities resurfaced. However, rather than resorting to physical violence and force (although there were some minor confrontations), Clay's citizenry opted to allow the Latter-day Saints to relocate peacefully and even offered to assist them in locating to a new region for settlement.

As early as March 1836, Church leaders in Missouri began searching out possible sites for permanent settlement in the sparsely populated region of "unincorporated" Ray County, situated to the north and east of Clay County. During the next several months, after making extensive explorations, Mormon leaders purchased property in the area of Shoal and Goose creeks, which included a one-mile-square plat (640 acres) in Mirable Township. The site later became known as Far West. With this acquisition, Mormons began moving to Far West and the surrounding area in significant numbers.

During the fall 1836 Missouri legislative session, Alexander W. Doniphan, Clay County's representative to the state legislature and the Mormons' principal attorney, introduced legislation proposing the creation of a county exclusively for the Mormons in the "unincorporated" portion of northern Ray County. However, as discussions progressed, Doniphan began to fear that the bill to organize one county exclusively for the Mormons might not pass, so he proposed establishing a second county—a "gentile" county for non-Mormons—directly north of the proposed Mormon county. The bill passed the Missouri legislature, and on December 29, 1836, Governor Lilburn W. Boggs signed it into law, creating Caldwell and Daviess counties, with Caldwell County being set aside for Mormon occupation. Although no written law or rule actually prescribed that Mormons could settle only in Caldwell County—like any citizen, Mormons had every right to settle wherever they chose—Missourians fully anticipated that the Mormons would confine themselves to Caldwell County.

In the minds of state and regional officials and the citizens in Missouri's northwest region, the establishment of a county exclusively for the Latter-day Saints appeared to solve "the Mormon problem," and for nearly two years (August 1836 to August 1838), relations between the Mormons and their non-Mormon neighbors stabilized. However, in reality, by creating Caldwell County for Mormon occupation, officials actually set up the conditions for a potentially greater conflict.

To understand why Mormon-Missouri relations deteriorated in 1838, it is important to understand four fundamental underlying causes that precipitated the conflict.

## CAUSE #1: JOSEPH SMITH AND THE MORMON LEADERSHIP ESTABLISH PERMANENT RESIDENCE IN FAR WEST

During the latter part of 1837, the Latter-day Saint movement was fractured by internal dissension in Ohio. At the heart of the agitation was not so much Mormonism in and of itself, but dissatisfaction with Joseph Smith and the temporal policies adopted by the Mormon leadership. The nationwide economic panic of 1837 inflated land prices, and the failure of the Church-backed Kirtland Safety Society Anti-Banking Company caused a significant, albeit relatively small number of disaffected Church members to question Joseph Smith's leadership and inspiration. Warren Parish (the Prophet's former secretary), John F. Boynton (a member of the Quorum of the Twelve), and Warren Cowdery (former Church recorder, editor of the *Latter Day Saints' Messenger and Advocate*, and member of the

The failure of the Church-owned banking institution known as the Kirtland Safety Society led to a crisis of faith among some leading members of the Church. In the end, the apostasy of some forced Joseph Smith to leave Kirtland and take up residence in Far West, Missouri.

Kirtland high council) were the leading and most influential detractors. But a considerable core of leading Mormon officials came under their influence, including Frederick G. Williams of the First Presidency; Luke and Lyman Johnson of the Twelve; Leonard Rich, Sylvester Smith, John Gould, John C. Gaylord, and Salmon Gee of the Seventy; and even Martin Harris, one of the Three Witnesses of the Book of Mormon. By January 1838, the Kirtland dissenters gained the upper hand in Kirtland, threatening the Church leadership with legal battles and personal threats against their lives. Seeing no other recourse, Joseph Smith, in company with Sidney Rigdon, fled Kirtland for Missouri in early January 1838. Following a two-month journey, they arrived in Far West in mid-March 1838.

However, the Prophet's move to Far West in 1838 sent a signal to the Missourians that the Mormon leadership was taking up a permanent position in Missouri. This did not sit well with the locals, who believed that Mormonism could be contained as long as the Mormon leadership and the headquarters of the Church remained in Ohio. Once Far West became the primary place of gathering, Missourians feared it would be only a matter of time before the Mormons would dominate the region.

## CAUSE #2: MORMON EXPANSION OUTSIDE CALDWELL COUNTY

With a county exclusively their own, Church members and new converts in the East, encouraged by the news that a region had been designated for Latter-day Saint settlement, began pouring in. Believing that the Mormon migration to Far West and the rest of Caldwell County would cause the county to fill up or be overrun,

Joseph Smith publicly declared in late 1837 the Church's proposition that other of the "upper counties"—probably referring to Daviess County—could support newcomers and that "other stakes" would be created and organized "in the regions round about."[2]

While Caldwell remained the principal gathering place, with Daviess County second, Mormons did not confine themselves to these two counties. In July 1838, LDS emigrants began purchasing property in the community of De Witt, located in Carroll County. In addition, Ray, Livingston, Clinton, and Chariton counties each had a share of Mormon occupants. Thus, with the expectation that an ever-growing number of Latter-day Saints would continue to immigrate and settle in Caldwell, and the fact that other Mormons were beginning to settle in the surrounding regions contrary to original agreements, Mormon phobia once again resurfaced. One Missouri reporter wrote: "The Mormons . . . agreed to settle in, and confine themselves to . . . the county of Caldwell; but they have violated that agreement, and are spreading over Davies[s], Clinton, Livingston, and Carroll." He also said that so many Mormons had moved into Daviess that it would not be long before the local settlers would be governed "by the Revelations of the great Prophet, Joe Smith, . . . hence their anxiety to rid themselves of [them]."[3]

The presence of the Prophet Joseph Smith in Far West was interpreted by local non-Mormons that the headquarters of the Church was now in northern Missouri—and that soon the despised Mormons would overrun not only Caldwell County but other counties as well, a possibility that was simply unacceptable to them.

## CAUSE #3: SIDNEY RIGDON'S SALT SERMON AND THE EXPULSION OF MORMON DISSENTERS FROM FAR WEST

Joseph Smith expected that Missouri would bring a respite from the internal opposition he had experienced in the Kirtland community. However, at the time of his arrival at Far West, the Church in Missouri was in the middle of an apostasy crisis of its own. Between March and May 1838, Oliver Cowdery, David Whitmer, John Whitmer, Jacob Whitmer, William E. McLellin, William W. Phelps, Frederick G. Williams, and Lyman Johnson—all leading elders— were the subject of Church discipline. While Phelps and Williams reconciled with the authorities, Cowdery, the Whitmer brothers, McLellin, and Johnson were formally cut off from the Church. Following their excommunication, the dissenters—with the exception of McLellin, who left and moved to Liberty—remained in Far

When the Saints took up residence in Daviess and other surrounding counties, it further enraged the locals, who felt that Mormons should have strictly confined themselves to only Caldwell County. This photo shows the town and temple site at Adam-ondi-Ahman.

Olivery Cowdery, assistant president of the Church and a Witness to the Book of Mormon, was excommunicated for apostasy by the high council in Far West, Missouri, on April 12, 1838. He was among several vocal opponents cut off from the Church that spring.

West, where they continued to stir up trouble. Fearing a repeat of Kirtland, an ultimatum was issued publicly and individually to the detractors that they were no longer welcome in Far West.

On June 17, 1838, during a worship service of the Saints at the public square, Sidney Rigdon delivered a scathing sermon, using as his text the words of Jesus from St. Matthew: "If the salt have lost his savour, . . . it is thenceforth good for nothing, but to be cast out, and to be trodden under foot of men" (Matt. 5:13), making it explicitly clear that the men would be expected to move from the county. The rhetorical threats made out against the dissenters produced the desired results, and within a few days the men left, taking up permanent residence with their families in Richmond, Ray County.

Unexpectedly, however, the episode involving the dissenters' expulsion opened the door to further troubles between Mormons and non-Mormons. Following their flight, these former Mormon leaders were quick to spread the news of their alleged mistreatment. The report of so-called abuse by Mormon leaders was evidence to the Missourians that Joseph Smith and his associates could not be trusted. Furthermore, it reconfirmed in the minds of the local citizens that the Latter-day Saints posed a genuine threat to the peace and security of the region.

## CAUSE #4: SIDNEY RIGDON'S JULY 4TH SPEECH

The Mormon Independence Day celebration held at the public square of Far West on July 4, 1838, proved to be another defining moment in connection with the Mormon expulsion from Missouri. The order of the day included a military parade, music, prayers, a flag ceremony, and the dedication and the laying of the four cornerstones for the proposed temple. These events, however, were upstaged by an articulate and passionate oration given by Sidney Rigdon. He used the occasion to eloquently recount the principles of freedom by which the founders established the government and the rights that religious societies are entitled under its provisions. Speaking in general terms, he also recounted the false reports circulated about Mormonism as well as the persecution and suffering experienced by the Church from its earliest beginnings.

In his closing statements, however, Rigdon's speech took on a different tone. Buoyed by the relative peace that had existed in northern Missouri since 1836, and secure in the notion that continued immigration would result in a steady increase in Mormon population, Rigdon announced that the Mormons would no longer suffer abuse at the hands of their enemies. "We have proved the world with kindness, we have suffered their abuse without cause, with patience, and have endured without resentment, until this day. . . . But from this day and this hour, we will suffer it no more." Rigdon's final words were words of warning. "That mob that comes on us to disturb us; it shall be between us and them a war of extermination, for we will follow them, till the last drop of their blood is spilled, or else they will have to exterminate us; for we will carry the seat of war to their own houses, and their own families, and one party or the other shall be destroyed."[4]

Looking back six years later, Jedediah M. Grant believed Rigdon's speech reignited the fire of Missouri anti-Mormon opposition. "[The oration] was the main auxiliary that fanned into a flame the burning wrath of the mobocratic portion of the Missourians. They now had an excuse, their former threats were renewed, and soon executed, [and] we were then . . . all made accountable for the acts of one man."[5] Brigham Young's hindsight concerning the occasion was similar to that of Grant's: "Elder Rigdon was the prime cause of our troubles in Missouri, by his fourth of July oration."[6]

## BEGINNING OF HOSTILITIES

Following Rigdon's Independence Day speech, Missourians living in the counties bordering Caldwell prepared to strike out against the Mormons. The first of outbreak of violence took place at Gallatin, the Daviess County seat, on August 6, 1838, on the occasion of the statewide elections. By this time a significant number of Latter-day Saints lived in Missouri counties other than Caldwell, the majority of them in Daviess, situated to the north. When a number of Mormon men turned out on the day of the election to exercise their right to vote at the polls, several Missourians put up some

On Sunday, June 17, 1838, Sidney Rigdon delivered an impassioned speech in Far West likening apostates to salt that had lost its savor and was good for nothing but to be cast out. The message to the dissenters was unmistakable—clear out or else. And so they did, eliciting the sympathy of the anti-Mormon population as they went.

Jedediah M. Grant reported that Sidney Rigdon's fiery July Fourth speech reignited the wrath of the Missourians against the Mormons.

resistance, and a bloody fight broke out. Being unarmed, the Mormon men used what means were available for their defense, including rocks, clubs, and an occasional butcher knife. The entire melee lasted only about two minutes, and fortunately no one on either side was killed, but there were plenty of cuts, bruises, and sore skulls. Although it is still unclear whether or not the Mormons ever voted, to the settlers living in the northern counties the incident was evidence that they could not live compatibly with their Mormon neighbors.

Mormon leaders at Far West responded immediately. Two Mormon companies from Caldwell County—one of which included Joseph Smith—went to Daviess County to ascertain details of the incident and to settle any differences. One contingent visited the home of Adam Black, a justice of the peace, to determine his intentions as a civil servant, and eventually they secured a signed statement from him that he would use his influence to preserve and maintain peace in the region. Within a few days, however, Black pressed charges of threat and intimidation against Joseph Smith and several other Mormon leaders. The events surrounding Black's encounter with the Mormons immediately spawned rumors and exaggerated reports about Mormon activities and intentions throughout much of northern Missouri. "Representations of these hostile movements of the Mormons were sent by express to the neighboring counties which created considerable excitement," wrote Reed Peck. The general cry from Daviess residents was "that the Mormons should be expelled from that county as it would be impossible to live in peace with them."[7] Volunteers from other counties were immediately called to come to their aid. The Mormon-Missouri war had begun.

On August 6, 1838, a brawl broke out between a small group of Mormons and some Missourians in the village and county seat of Gallatin. This dust-up was exaggerated by rumor and alarmed the populace on both sides.

## DAVIESS COUNTY VIGILANTISM (AUGUST THROUGH MID-SEPTEMBER 1838)

Following the Adam Black incident, throughout the remainder of August and much of September, vigilante forces from Daviess, Livingston,

Carroll, and Saline counties began intimidating and harassing Mormon settlers throughout the region but primarily those living in Daviess County. "A mob of about three hundred armed men . . . made prisoners of some of the Mormons, shooting and driving away their cattle, and threatening to exterminate or expel them from the county unless they would deny their faith," John P. Greene reported.[8] Hoping to be assured of greater protection from hostile bands, the majority of Mormon families living in outlying settlements in Daviess as well as the adjacent counties moved closer to Adam-ondi-Ahman and established temporary homes and shelters.

On August 30, when news of the illegal activities by the local county regulators reached Missouri officials, B. M. Lisle, adjutant general of the Missouri state militia, ordered David R. Atchison—a Liberty resident and major-general of the state militia's 3rd Division—to call out troops and march to Daviess to put down the disturbances.[9] Atchison was assisted by his law partner and fellow militia officer, Alexander W. Doniphan, and by Hiram G. Parks, Ray County militia commander. For nearly two weeks, Atchison, Doniphan, and Parks and their militia companies reconnoitered in Caldwell and Daviess counties, marching and countermarching. By mid-September they succeeded disbanding the Missouri miscreants and eventually reestablished order in the county.

General David Rice Atchison, a major-general in the Missouri State militia, was ordered to call out troops to restore peace in Daviess County. With the assistance of Alexander W. Doniphan and Hiram G. Parks, both militia officers, order was restored, but only for a short time.

To maintain the peace, Atchison assigned two companies of approximately one hundred men under the command of Parks to remain in the region "until confidence and tranquility should be restored."[10] The Mormons, now of the opinion that stability had been permanently restored, anticipated no further conflict. "We thought that the matter was settled and we all went about our business," remembered William Cooper.[11]

## EXPULSION OF THE MORMONS FROM DE WITT, CARROLL COUNTY (OCTOBER 1–10, 1838)

Following the scene of conflict in Daviess, vigilante forces shifted their field of operations to De Witt, located approximately seventy miles from Far West in the southeast section of Carroll

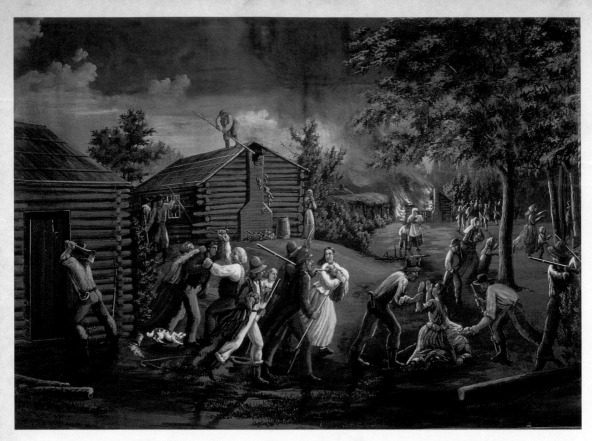

Notwithstanding a temporary peace in Daviess County, mob action soon shifted some seventy miles to the southeast. From October 1–10, 1838, mobs surrounded and harassed the Saints in the small community of De Witt. When Governor Boggs refused to intervene, the Saints were forced to surrender and evacuate.

County. As early as June 1838, Mormons began settling in De Witt. However, their presence sparked immediate opposition, and throughout the summer, county regulators used a number of means, albeit unsuccessfully, to coerce the Mormons to relocate.

Beginning on October 1, a vigilante force of about three hundred citizens from Carroll, Howard, Saline, and Clay counties began a siege of the settlement, harassing the Mormons "by day & by night by Scouting parties of the mob in & about Dewitt," wrote John Murdock.[12] However, under the command of Colonel George M. Hinkle, a commissioned officer in the state militia and a Latter-day Saint, the Mormons courageously defended the community. In the meantime, on October 6, Ray County militia commander Hiram G. Parks arrived on the scene with two military companies intent on settling the difficulties. But shortly after his arrival, Parks informed the Mormons that the greater part of his troops had "mutinied and were mobocratic" and could not be depended on to enforce the law or defend the Mormons. He was forced to withdraw his troops, he said, for fear that they would join the mob.[13]

About this same time, A. L. Caldwell, a local citizen sympathetic to the Mormons, returned from Jefferson City, where he had met with Governor Boggs and requested his assistance. Caldwell indicated that the governor was unsympathetic toward the

Mormons and refused to intervene. "The quarrel was between the Mormons and the mob," he reported Boggs as saying, and they "might fight it out."[14] Sadly, on October 10, following a ten-day standoff, Hinckle surrendered to the vigilante forces and signed an agreement that the Mormons would leave the community. Within days, approximately four hundred Latter-day Saints abandoned their homes and property and moved to Caldwell County.[15]

## EXPULSION OF THE NON-MORMONS FROM DAVIESS COUNTY (MID-OCTOBER, 1838)

Following the removal of the Mormons from De Witt, vigilantes in Daviess County immediately set out to recommence operations to bring about the wholesale removal of the Mormons from that region. The cry of the expulsionist forces was to drive the Mormons "from Daviess to Caldwell, and from Caldwell to Hell."[16] The anti-Mormon antagonists also supposed they had little to fear, believing the Mormons would give them only moderate resistance. Furthermore, they were confident most of the civil officers and members of the state militia were actually on their side and would not intervene or attempt to check them in their activities. On the other hand, knowing they could not afford to give up any of their claims in Daviess, Mormon leaders moved to oppose and halt additional incursions by vigilante groups. Thereafter, Mormon officials and militia officers initiated active, rather than passive, defensive warfare.

On October 18, three Mormon companies at Adam-ondi-Ahman launched offensives at Millport, Gallatin, and the region known as Grindstone Fork. In each of these locales, the Mormon companies confiscated household items and personal property of the known anti-Mormon agitators and ringleaders, then set fire to their homes or establishments. In total, a dozen or more buildings were burned in Millport (where most of the leading vigilante leaders lived), at least four were destroyed in Gallatin, and an unknown number were destroyed in the Grindstone Fork area. The message was clear—the Mormons would no longer tolerate hostile activities against them.

Emboldened by their success, Mormon guards in Daviess County continued the siege beyond what was originally intended, which had been selective in nature and targeted against known non-Mormon agitators as well as the settlements that harbored them. However, under the direction and encouragement of Adam-ondi-Ahman's leaders, especially Lyman Wight, Mormon

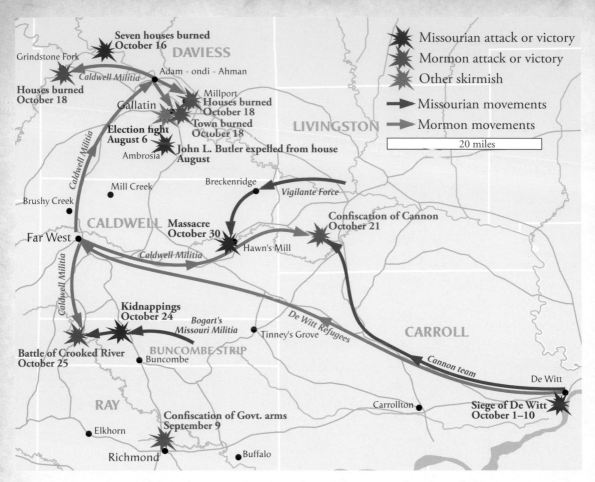

Seven houses burned
October 16

DAVIESS

Grindstone Fork

Caldwell Militia

Adam - ondi - Ahman

Millport

Houses burned
October 18

Town burned
October 18

LIVINGSTON

Houses burned
October 18

Gallatin

Election fight
August 6

John L. Butler expelled from house
August

Ambrosia

Mill Creek

Breckenridge

Vigilante Force

Brushy Creek

CALDWELL

Massacre
October 30

Confiscation of Cannon
October 21

Far West

Caldwell Militia

Hawn's Mill

Caldwell Militia

Kidnappings
October 24

Bogart's
Missouri Militia

De Witt Refugees

Tinney's Grove

CARROLL

Battle of Crooked River
October 25

BUNCOMBE STRIP

Buncombe

Cannon team

De Witt

RAY

Elkhorn

Confiscation of Govt. arms
September 9

Carrollton

Siege of De Witt
October 1–10

Richmond

Buffalo

Missourian attack or victory

Mormon attack or victory

Other skirmish

Missourian movements

Mormon movements

20 miles

There were a number of conflicts between Mormons and non-Mormons across northern Missouri that rightfully led to this being termed "the Mormon War." In the end, the conflict resulted in the expulsion of the Saints from the state and the confiscation of their property.

troops in Daviess County continued to patrol the county, confiscating property of innocent civilians and anyone considered to pose a threat to the Mormons. With no military presence in the area, lawlessness prevailed on both sides. John D. Lee wrote that during this time Daviess County was in complete disorder. "Armed men roamed in bands all over . . . Daviess . . . both Mormons and Gentiles were under arms, and doing injury to each other when occasion offered. The burning of houses, farms, and stacks of grain was generally indulged in by each party. Lawlessness prevailed, and pillage was the rule."[17] In short, both sides conducted indiscriminate acts of intimidation and hostility against the other.

By the end of October, fearing that the Mormons would eventually prevail, nearly all the remaining non-Mormon residents fled to nearby Livingston County, while vigilante forces backed off, expecting regulators from other locales or the state militia to come to their aid. Meanwhile, Mormon settlers in the county withdrew to Adam-ondi-Ahman to fortify the settlement.[18]

# BATTLE OF CROOKED RIVER
## (OCTOBER 25, 1838)

The standoff in Daviess County between the Mormons and the Missouri vigilantes shifted the seat of hostilities from Daviess County in the north to Ray County in the south. Fearful that the Mormons would extend their depredations outside Daviess, Captain Samuel Bogart of the Ray County militia received permission from his superiors on October 23 for his company, composed of thirty-five men, to patrol the Caldwell-Ray County line with the purpose of intercepting any type of Mormon incursion, even though the Latter-day Saints had no such intentions.

Bogart's actions, however, reveal that he was more intent on conducting hostile activities than on protecting civilians. On October 24, Bogart's company appeared in the southern portion of Caldwell County, where he and his men threatened and intimidated innocent Latter-day Saints living in the area. The Ray commander also accosted three Mormons—Nathan Pinkham Jr., William Seely, and Addison Green—taking them prisoner before bivouacking at a strategic position on Crooked River, just inside the Ray County line.

In the meantime, Mormon messengers quickly made their way to Far West, bringing word of Bogart's activities. Upon learning that three Mormon men had been taken hostage, Mormon officials acted immediately to rescue them. To place a stamp of civil authority on the campaign, Caldwell County Judge Elias Higbee commissioned Mormon Apostle David W. Patten (also known as "Captain Fear Not") to organize and lead a company of Caldwell militia to track down the perpetrators and rescue the prisoners.

During the early morning hours of October 25, Patten's company of sixty volunteers discovered Bogart's position. Upon their approach, John Lockart, a picket guard in the Ray contingent, shot and picked off Patterson O'Banion (sometimes referred to as Patrick O'Bannion), who was at the front of the Mormon company. Heavy fighting ensued shortly thereafter. "The first we knew they commenced a brisk fire upon our whole body, shooting down many of our best brethren all around us and hollering so that we had no other course to take but to defend ourselves the best way we could," wrote Parley P. Pratt.[19] Commander Patten was also caught in the barrage and was an easy target, receiving a wound that later proved fatal. "[He] wore a white blanket coat which made him a conspicuous mark," Charles C. Rich recalled.[20]

From their defensive position on the east side of riverbank (which also served as a breastwork), the Ray militia had a

During the pre-dawn hours of October 25, 1838, a group of Latter-day Saints in the capacity of militia—led by David W. Patten of the Quorum of the Twelve—engaged a hostile company of Ray County militia at Crooked River. In the ensuing battle, three Mormons and one Missourian were killed. Among the casualties was Elder Patten.

distinct strategic advantage. However, the Mormons clearly had the superior fighting force, outnumbering Bogart's company by nearly two to one. As the battle ensued, the Mormons attacked from three different positions, which enabled them to gradually advance and eventually overpower the Missourians, forcing them to retreat across the river. The Missourians subsequently fled in all directions.

Although the Caldwell militia succeeded in routing Bogart's troops and in rescuing the Mormon prisoners, a number of casualties resulted on both sides. Seven members of the Caldwell company were wounded—Eli Chase, James Hendricks, Curtis Hodge, Joseph Holbrook, Arthur Milliken, William Seeley, and Norman Shearer—and three died in the attack or soon after (Patterson O'Banion, David W. Patten, and Gideon Carter). The Ray militia suffered one casualty, Moses Rowland, and half a dozen others were wounded.

On October 27, two days after the battle, word reached Governor Boggs in Jefferson City that the Mormons had attacked and completely annihilated Bogart's company. Although the reports were spurious and greatly exaggerated, Boggs perceived that the Mormons had perpetrated the conflict and were in open rebellion against the state of Missouri by deliberately attacking the state militia. He viewed this act as treasonous, as evidenced by his statement: "The Mormons [are] in the attitude of an open

Brigham Young University Museum of Art, gift of the grandchildren of C.C.A. Christensen, 1970.

and avowed defiance of the laws, and of having made war upon the people of this state." Such actions on the part of the Latter-day Saints led him to justify his final solution to the Mormon problem—full-scale expulsion—"the Mormons must be treated as enemies and must be exterminated or driven from the State if necessary for the public peace." [21]

## HAWN'S MILL (OCTOBER 30, 1838)

The Mormon "cleansing" of Daviess County non-Mormons during the last half of October, coupled with the erroneous reports that Samuel Bogart's forces had been routed and then annihilated at Crooked River on October 25, sent a signal to vigilante groups in northern Missouri that

more extreme measures would have to be undertaken in order to restore local control and bring about complete Mormon submission. Anti-Mormon forces—principally from Livingston County, assisted by a number of Daviess refugees and a handful of community regulators from other locales—were the first to respond to the Mormon strikes. They did so in a retaliatory fashion by assaulting an innocent civilian population at Hawn's Mill in eastern Caldwell County. In writing about the Missourians who carried out the tragedy at Hawn's Mill, nineteenth-century Missouri historian Reburn I. Holcombe (writing under the pen name of Burr Joyce) wrote:

Lilburn W. Boggs served as governor of Missouri from 1836–1840. In October 1838, he issued the "Extermination Order" that brought incalculable suffering to the Latter-day Saints. Boggs would live out his last days in California, as Parley P. Pratt declared, "with the mark of Cain upon his brow."

> Nearly all of the men were citizens of Living-ston County. Perhaps twenty were from Daviess,

Hawn's Mill was a small settlement in eastern Caldwell County comprised mainly of Latter-day Saints and named for Jacob Hawn, a non-Mormon millwright in the area. The actions of the Mormons against the Missourians in Daviess County brought terrible retribution against the innocent Saints who were at the mill when the Livingston County and Daviess County men attacked the peaceful settlement.

from whence they had been driven by the Mormons during the troubles in that county a few weeks previously. The Daviess County men were very bitter against the Mormons, and vowed the direst vengeance on the entire sect. It did not matter whether or not the Mormons at the mill had taken any part in the disturbance which had occurred [in Daviess]; it was enough that they were Mormons. The Livingston men became thoroughly imbued with the same spirit, and all were eager for the raid, . . . feel[ing] an extraordinary sympathy for the outrages suffered by their neighbors.[22]

In the days immediately preceding the attack, anti-Mormon regulators from Livingston County visited Hawn's Mill, issuing threats and confiscating a number of the settlers' guns, weapons, and ammunition. They also intercepted, detained, and harassed several Mormon immigrant companies passing through Livingston before allowing them to proceed to Caldwell. Such actions clearly demonstrated their intentions to be ultimately hostile. In spite of the bullying, life at the mill went on as usual, although community members organized a guard detail to watch for any suspicious activity.

It is not known precisely when the decision was made by the Livingston and Daviess county regulators to carry out the deadly assault at Hawn's Mill, but once the final plan was put in place, they attempted to legitimize the operation by organizing under the guise of a regional militia. On October 29, more than two hundred men assembled a few miles north of the mill settlement, where they made final preparations. The following day, around three o'clock, the strike commenced.

The attackers came upon the settlement completely unnoticed and took quick action. When the first shots were fired, the women and children scattered into the woods and nearby homes, while most of the men darted into an unfinished blacksmith shop, where they had stockpiled a few weapons. The Mormons held off their attackers for several minutes, but the Missourians eventually succeeded in surrounding the shop at close range. As they did so, the fire became more deadly. "Seeing no prospect before us but death, the mob manifesting all malice possible and would not listen to our cries and seemed determined to murder us all, we thought it advisable for us to make our escape," wrote Ellis Ames.[23] As the men left the shop, bullets whizzed from every direction, hitting the Mormon men as they tried to run for cover.

When the firing from the blacksmith shop stopped, the regulators cautiously approached the structure to investigate and

The attack on Hawn's Mill by the mob was not a random act of rage, but rather a premeditated assault and a calculated act of vengeance and plunder.

determine the extent of the Mormon losses. Once inside, the Missourians continued their hostilities, abusing the wounded and killing others. The dead were also stripped of their salvageable clothing and footwear. After securing the settlement, the vigilantes ransacked the homes and temporary shelters, taking household items, food, and animals. The entire assault on the mill lasted between thirty and sixty minutes.

Fifteen Mormons were killed during the attack or died shortly afterward. Two others died within a few weeks, making seventeen total casualties. Another fifteen were wounded. The dead were buried the following day, October 31. Fourteen of the Mormon victims were buried in a dry well, including Elias Benner, John Byers, Alexander Campbell, Simon Cox, Josiah Fuller, Austin Hammer, John Lee, Thomas McBride, Levi N. Merrick, William Napier/ Naper, George S. Richards (age fifteen), Sardius Smith (age ten), Warren Smith, and John York. Hiram Abbot lived five weeks following the attack. Charles Merrick (age nine) was wounded while fleeing from the blacksmith shop and died four weeks later. The final fatality, Benjamin Lewis, was buried in a grave of his own by his brother David Lewis. Historians have generally concluded that the attack made by the Livingston militia on the Hawn's Mill community was associated with the October 27 "Extermination Order" of Governor Lilburn W. Boggs. However, historical sources actually indicate no connection with the governor's directive whatsoever, since the Livingston marauders did not even learn about the order until October 31, the day following the attack.[24]

Among those brutally murdered by the mob was ten-year-old Sardius Smith. He was discovered hiding beneath the bellows of the blacksmith shop and was shot at point-blank range.

Opposite Bottom: Major-General Samuel D. Lucas assumed command of the Missouri militia forces near Far West when the governor relieved General Atchison of the duty. Lucas proved much less sympathetic to the Mormons than his predecessor and demanded that they comply with the governor's order to leave the state.

# THE MORMON DEFENSE OF FAR WEST (OCTOBER 28–31, 1838)

The day after the assault at Hawn's Mill, fourteen of the Mormon victims were buried in a dry well that served as a mass grave.

The executive order issued by Governor Lilburn W. Boggs calling for the removal of the Mormons was executed by Major-General Samuel D. Lucas of the 4th Division of the Missouri militia and the commander of the troops from Jackson and Lafayette counties. The day before issuing the order, the governor relieved Major-General David R. Atchison of his command of the state militia in the Northern District. Atchison's release probably stemmed from the fact that he had served as legal counsel to Joseph Smith and was at least partially sympathetic to the Mormons. Boggs replaced Atchison with Major-General John B. Clark of Howard County. But since Clark was not on the scene to take charge, Lucas *assumed* command.

Less than three days after the executive order was issued, approximately 2,500 state troops had assembled near Goose Creek (about a mile south of Far West) to prepare for a final all-out offensive against the Mormons. At the same time the state troops were assembling, the Mormons were digging in and preparing a bulwark on the southern outskirts of Far West. "[We] formed in line of battle, in single column," Ebenezer Robinson remembered, "[and] stretched out as far as we could." He further remarked that because the men were stationed several feet apart, "to an observer at a distance, we made a very formidable appearance."[25]

Bottom: Samuel D. Lucas—courtesy of the Church History Library

On October 31, a messenger from Hawn's Mill arrived at Far West with information about the massacre that had taken place the previous afternoon. News of the tragedy rocked the entire Mormon community and further demonstrated to the Latter-day Saints the extent to which the anti-Mormon element would go to in order to bring about the Mormon removal. The slaughter also brought the Mormon leaders to the shocking realization that they were in a "no win" situation. Although they could choose to defend themselves and possibly hold out for a short period of time, this would result only in the additional loss of life and Mormon resources.

Recognizing the gravity of the situation and the distinct advantage of the Missouri troops, Church leaders concluded that a settlement or treaty must be reached.

On October 31, 1838, George M. Hinkle, the Mormon commander, turned Joseph Smith and four other men over to General Lucas and his officers. The following day, Hyrum Smith and Amasa Lyman were taken into custody. These arrests ultimately led to the incarceration of Joseph Smith and five others in Liberty Jail during the winter of 1838–1839.

When a five-man Mormon delegation consisting of William W. Phelps, Arthur Morrison, Reed Peck, John Corrill, and George M. Hinkle met with Lucas and his staff at his encampment, the militia general read Boggs's October 27 directive and issued four ultimatums: (1) the Mormons must give up their leaders; (2) those individuals who had taken up arms must turn over their property as compensation for the cost of the war; (3) the entire

Joseph Smith and four other men were arrested on October 31, 1838, an arrest that led to the Prophet's incarcertion in Liberty Jail.

Mormon population must leave the state; and (4) Mormon defenders must surrender their weapons.

The Mormon peace delegation returned to Far West to discuss the conditions. John Corrill later recalled: "We immediately went into town and collected Joseph Smith, Jr., Sidney Rigden [*sic*], Lyman Wight, Parley P. Pratt, and George W. Robertson [Robinson] together, and told them what the Governor's order and General Lucas required."[26] A short while later, the Mormon peace delegation returned, accompanied by the Mormon leaders. A few words were said, and the two parties shook hands, whereupon Hinkle remarked, "Here general are the prisoners I agreed to deliver to you."[27]

## THE MORMON SURRENDER, MILITIA OCCUPATION, AND THE RICHMOND PRELIMINARY COURT HEARINGS (NOVEMBER 1–29, 1838)

On the morning of November 1, General Lucas conducted the final surrender formalities at Far West's public square and made additional arrests, which included Hyrum Smith and Amasa Lyman. (A second formal surrender was conducted at Adam-ondi-Ahman on November 9.) Later that evening Lucas made a rash and hasty decision to hold court-martial proceedings for Joseph Smith and the six other prisoners on the charge of treason—a capital offense. The deliberation did not last long; a guilty verdict was rendered, and Alexander Doniphan was ordered to execute the men the following morning. However, Doniphan considered the action illegal and refused to obey the order, which led Lucas to reconsider his decision and to ultimately decide to keep all seven Mormon men in custody until they could be turned over to the appropriate civil authorities.

During the forenoon of November 2, a heavily guarded wagon containing the seven Mormon prisoners pulled into Far West. Moses Wilson, a brigadier-general, was assigned to take the Mormon prisoners to Independence while Lucas finalized the surrender. Lucas remained overnight, leaving Far West the next day in order to catch up with Wilson. On the afternoon of Sunday, November 4, Lucas and Wilson arrived in Independence with the Mormon leaders. Here they waited for word regarding where a civil hearing would be held.

On November 4, Major-General John B. Clark arrived at Far West, where he supervised the final activities of the Mormon

Following a November 1, 1838, court-martial hearing, General Samuel D. Lucas ordered Alexander W. Doniphan (above) to take Joseph Smith and the other Mormon prisoners to the public square the next morning and shoot them. Doniphan refused to obey the illegal order, considering it "cold-blooded murder," and he threatened Lucas with legal action if the prisoners were executed. Doniphan's courage spared the Mormon leaders.

surrender and conducted additional arrests. The following day he dispatched a small guard to Independence with orders for Lucas to turn over Joseph Smith and the six other prisoners so they could be taken to Richmond for examination. They arrived in Richmond on November 9, where they were put into a vacant log house north of Richmond's public square and courthouse, placed under guard, and chained together in heavy irons. For three weeks the log house served as the ad hoc jail for the seven Mormon men.

Meanwhile, on the afternoon of Tuesday, November 6, General Clark left Far West and marched to Richmond with forty-six additional Mormon men he had arrested and taken into custody. Clark's company arrived at the Ray County seat on November 9, at which time he discharged the remainder of his division, with the exception of a small force that he detained to guard the entire number of Mormon prisoners who had been brought to Richmond for the court examination.

The Richmond court of inquiry, presided over by Fifth District Circuit Court Judge Austin A. King, convened on November 12 and continued through November 29. The purpose of the hearing was to examine the charges levied against the Mormons and to determine if there was probable cause to bind the defendants over for trial. Thomas Burch and William Wood prosecuted in behalf of the state, while the Mormon prisoners were represented by Alexander Doniphan, Amos Rees, and Peter H. Burnett. During the course of the hearing, eleven additional Mormon prisoners were arrested and charged, bringing the total number of Mormon defendants to sixty-four.

Following nearly three weeks of testimony, the court released twenty-nine of the sixty-four Mormon defendants. Judge King determined that sufficient evidence existed to bind thirty-five over for trial, although they were allowed to post bail and were released. He also ruled that there was sufficient evidence to charge five men—Parley P. Pratt, Norman Shearer, Darwin Chase, Luman Gibbs, and Morris Phelps—in the death of Moses Rowland, which had occurred during the attack at Crooked River. Since the charge of murder was non-bailable, these five men were ordered to remain confined in the Richmond Jail until their final hearing convened. (In March 1839, King Follett was incarcerated with the Richmond prisoners on different charges.) Finally, probable cause was found against Joseph Smith, Sidney Rigdon, Hyrum Smith, Lyman Wight, Alexander McCrae, and Caleb Baldwin on the charge of treason—also a non-bailable offense—for acts committed in Daviess County. However, because there was no jail in Daviess, King ordered the men be taken to Liberty Jail in Clay County to await their court appearance. The six Mormon leaders were quickly transferred to Liberty, where they arrived on December 1 to begin their confinement.[28]

## LIBERTY JAIL AND RICHMOND JAIL PRISONERS

There is sufficient historical evidence to conclude that Governor Lilburn W. Boggs and Judge Austin A. King never intended to fully prosecute Joseph Smith and the other Mormon prisoners. At the completion of the Richmond hearing in late November, as the Mormon prisoners were being taken to Liberty Jail, Hyrum Smith later reported that one of the officers in charge informed them that "the Judge declared his intention to keep us in jail until all the 'Mormons' were driven from the state. He also said that the Judge had further declared that if he let us out before the 'Mormons' had left the state, . . . there would be [a] . . . fuss kicked up." Hyrum's reporting continues:

Judge Austin A. King presided over hearings for the purpose of determining if the Latter-day Saint prisoners should be bound over for trial. While some were released, a number were charged with non-bailable crimes, including murder and treason.

> The jailer [at Liberty Jail], Samuel Tillery, Esq., told us . . . that the whole plan was concocted by the governor down to the lowest judge in that upper country. . . . He told us that the governor was now ashamed of the whole transaction and would be glad to set us at liberty if he dared do it. "But," said he, "you need not be concerned, for the governor has laid a plan for your release. He also said that Squire Birch [*sic*] . . . was appointed to be circuit judge on the circuit passing through Daviess county, and that he (Birch) was instructed to fix the papers, so that we would be sure to be clear from any incumbrance [*sic*] in a very short time.[29]

Joseph Smith, Hyrum Smith, Alexander McRae, Caleb Baldwin, and Lyman Wight were incarcerated in the jail at Liberty, Clay County, Missouri, from December 1, 1838, until April 6, 1839. Sidney Rigdon was released in February 1839. Historical evidence shows that these men were judicial hostages, held to insure that the Latter-day Saints left the state.

In short, Boggs and the lower court judges instigated a plan whereby once the main body of Mormons complied with the order to leave the state, the leaders would be released. This is indeed what took place. On April 6, 1839, following a four-month incarceration in Liberty, Joseph and Hyrum Smith, Lyman Wight, Alexander McRae, and Caleb Baldwin were transported to Gallatin for their trial. (Sidney Rigdon had secured a release in February.) During the hearing, which lasted three days (April 9–11), the defendants successfully petitioned and secured a change of venue to Columbia, Boone County, Missouri. On April 16, while en route, Sheriff William Morgan, the officer in charge of the transport, allowed the Mormon prisoners to escape. Morgan told the men that Judge Burch had instructed him to let them go. Six days later, the escapees crossed over the Mississippi River, joining the main body of Saints, who had assembled in Quincy.[30]

The experience of the Mormon inmates incarcerated in Richmond was somewhat similar to that of the Liberty Jail prisoners. In late May, after nearly a six-month confinement, Judge Austin A. King granted Parley P. Pratt, Morris Phelps, Luman Gibbs, and King Follett a change of venue, also to Columbia. (Norman Shearer and Darwin Chase were released in April.) However, unlike their Liberty counterparts, the four remaining prisoners were not released en route and were incarcerated in the Boone

County Jail. On July 4, impatient over the constant court delays, Pratt, Phelps, and Follett broke out of jail. Pratt and Phelps successfully escaped and made their way to Quincy, but Follett was recaptured. He remained in jail until late September, when his case was heard and he was acquitted and released. Luman Gibbs, who by this time had apostatized, remained incarcerated until November, when his case was dismissed.[31]

## INTERPRETATION OF 'EXTERMINATED'

Contrary to popular belief by many, among them even some Mormon historians, the governor's "Extermination Order" was not meant to authorize and license the state militia or its citizens to openly kill or eradicate the Latter-day Saint population. Although Boggs did not like the Mormons, he was not a butcher and did not condone the unnecessary taking of human life. In a report issued to the Missouri House of Representatives, Boggs himself stated that the order and call-up of troops was issued "to prevent the effusion of blood."[32] Significantly, the first definition of the word *exterminate* as defined in Webster's 1828 dictionary reads, "to drive from within the limits or borders."[33] Given this definition, the order should correctly be interpreted to read that the Mormons "must be exterminated or *[in other words]* driven from the State . . . for the public peace." Thus, Governor Boggs was calling for the removal of the Mormons by the militia, not their death sentence.

Elder Parley P. Pratt was among those who had participated in the Battle of Crooked River. Because of the death of Moses Rowland, a Missourian, Pratt was among those charged with murder and incarcerated at Richmond, Missouri. After being moved to Boone County, Parley and his fellow prisoner, Morris Phelps, escaped and made their way to the Saints in Illinois.

## EXTERMINATION ORDER RESCINDED

In the spirit of goodwill and reconciliation, on June 25, 1976, Missouri Governor Christopher S. Bond formally rescinded the executive order issued by his predecessor 138 years earlier. The document reads as follows:

> WHEREAS, on October 27, 1838, the Governor of the State of Missouri, Lilburn W. Boggs, issued

an order call for the extermination or expulsion of Mormons from the State of Missouri; and

WHEREAS, Governor Boggs' order clearly contravened the rights to life, liberty, property and religious freedom as guaranteed by the Constitution of the United States, as well as the Constitution of the States of Missouri; and

WHEREAS, in this Bicentennial year as we reflect on our nation's heritage, the exercise of religious freedom is without question one of the basic tenets of our free democratic republic;

NOW, THEREFORE, I, CHRISTOPHER S. BOND, Governor of the States of Missouri, by virtue of the authority vested in me by the Constitution and the laws of the State of Missouri, do hereby order as follows:

On June 25, 1976, Missouri Governor Christopher S. Bond rescinded the "Extermination Order" in a spirit of apology and reconciliation.

EXECUTIVE OFFICE
STATE OF MISSOURI
JEFFERSON CITY

CHRISTOPHER S. BOND
GOVERNOR

FILED
JUN 25 1976

SECRETARY OF STATE

EXECUTIVE ORDER

WHEREAS, on October 27, 1838, the Governor of the State of Missouri, Lilburn W. Boggs, issued an order calling for the extermination or expulsion of Mormons from the State of Missouri; and

WHEREAS, Governor Boggs' order clearly contravened the rights to life, liberty, property and religious freedom as guaranteed by the Constitution of the United States, as well as the Constitution of the State of Missouri; and

WHEREAS, in this Bicentennial year as we reflect on our nation's heritage, the exercise of religious freedom is without question one of the basic tenets of our free democratic republic;

NOW, THEREFORE, I, CHRISTOPHER S. BOND, Governor of the State of Missouri, by virtue of the authority vested in me by the Constitution and the laws of the State of Missouri, do hereby order as follows:

Expressing on behalf of all Missourians our deep regret for the injustice and undue suffering which was caused by this 1838 order, I hereby rescind Executive Order Number 44 dated October 27, 1838, issued by Governor Lilburn W. Boggs.

Page 2

EOF:   I have hereunto set my hand and caused to be affixed the great seal of the State of Missouri in the City of Jefferson on this 25th day of June, 1976.

GOVERNOR

ATE

Expressing on behalf of all Missourians our deep regret for the injustice and undue suffering which was caused by this 1838 order, I hereby rescind Executive Order Number 44 dated October 27, 1838, issued by Governor Lilburn W. Boggs.

IN WITNESS WHEREOF: I have hereunto set my hand and caused to be affixed the great seal of the State of Missouri in the City of Jefferson on this 25th day of June, 1976.

Christopher S. Bond [signed][34]

# Endnotes

1 Lilburn W. Boggs to John B. Clark, October 27, 1838, in *Document Containing the Correspondence, Orders, &C. In Relation to the Disturbances with the Mormons; And the Evidence Given Before the Hon. Austin A. King, Judge of the Fifth Judicial Circuit of the State of Missouri, at the Court-House in Richmond, in a Criminal Court of Inquiry, Begun November 12, 1838 on the Trial of Joseph Smith, Jr., and Others, for High Treason and Other Crimes Against the State* (Fayette, MO: Boon's Lick Democrat, 1841), 61 (hereafter cited as *Document*).

2 *Elders' Journal of the Church of the Latter Day Saints* 1, no. 18 (November 1837): 28. See also D&C 115:17–18.

3 "The Mormons," *Missouri Argus* (St. Louis, MO), September 27, 1838. The article, dated September 14, first appeared in the *Western Star* (Liberty, MO), publication date not known.

4 Sidney Rigdon, *Oration Delivered by Mr. S. Rigdon, on the 4th of July, 1838, at Far West, Caldwell County, Missouri* (Far West, MO: Printed at the Journal Office, 1838), 12. The entire document has since been published in Peter Crawley, "Two Rare Missouri Documents," *BYU Studies* 14, no. 4 (Summer 1974): 517–527.

5 Jedediah M. Grant, *Collection of Facts, Relative to the Course Taken By Elder Sidney Rigdon, in the States of Ohio, Missouri, Illinois, and Pennsylvania* (Philadelphia: Brown, Bicking & Gilbert, 1844), 11–12.

6 "Continuation of Elder Rigdon's Trial," *Times and Seasons* 5, no. 18 (1 October 1844), 667.

7 Reed Peck, "A Sketch of Mormon History," manuscript, 65, Henry E. Huntington Library, San Marino, California.

8 John P. Greene, *Facts Relative to the Expulsion of the Mormons or Latter Day Saints from the State of Missouri, under the "Exterminating Order"* (Cincinnati: R. P. Brooks, 1839), 19.

9 B. M. Lisle to David R. Atchison, August 30, 1838, in *Document*, 20.

10 David R. Atchison to Lilburn W. Boggs, September 20, 1838, in *Document*, 27; also in Joseph Smith Jr., *History of The Church of Jesus Christ of Latter-day Saints*, ed. B. H. Roberts, 2d ed., rev. 7 vols. (Salt Lake City: Deseret Book, 1971), 3:81–82 (hereafter cited as *History of the Church*).

11 Vinson Knight to William Cooper, February 3, 1839, typescript, Church History Library, Salt Lake City, Utah. For a more extensive examination of the August–September 1838 difficulties, see Alexander L. Baugh, "The War Begins: Conflict in Daviess County, August–September," in *A Call to Arms: The 1838 Mormon Defense of Northern Missouri* (Provo, UT: Joseph Fielding Smith Institute for Latter-day Saint History and BYU Studies, 2000), 47–64.

12 John Murdock, Petition, in Clark V. Johnson, ed., *Mormon Redress Petitions: Documents of the 1833–1838 Missouri Conflict* (Provo, UT: Religious Studies Center, Brigham Young University, 1992), 503.

13 *History of the Church*, 3:158.

14 Joseph Smith, "Extract, From the Private Journal of Joseph Smith, Jr." *Times and Seasons* 1, no. 1 (November 1839): 3; see also *History of the Church*, 3:157.

15 For a more extensive examination of the expulsion of the Mormons from De Witt, see Baugh, "The Mormon Defense of De Witt," in *A Call to Arms*, 65–81.

16 "Memorial of a Committee to the State Legislature of Missouri in Behalf of the Citizens of Caldwell County," in *History of the Church*, 3:420; also cited in Johnson, *Mormon Redress Petitions*, 111, 403.

17 John D. Lee, *Mormonism Unveiled; Including the Remarkable Life and Confessions of the Late Mormon Bishop, John D. Lee; and Complete Life of Brigham Young, Embracing a History of Mormonism From Its Inception Down to the Present Time, With an Exposition of the Secret History, Signs, Symbols, and Crimes of the Mormon Church. Also the True Story of the Horrible Butchery Known as the Mountain Meadows Massacre* (St. Louis: Moffatt Publishing Co., 1881), 70.

18 For a more extensive examination of the Mormon expulsion of the non-Mormons from Daviess County in mid-October 1838, see Baugh, "The Mormon Defense of Daviess County, October 1838," in *A Call to Arms*, 83–98.

19 Parley P. Pratt, *History of the Late Persecution Inflicted by the State of Missouri Upon the Mormons, in which Ten Thousand American Citizens Were Robbed, Plundered, and Driven From the State, and Many Others Imprisoned, Martyred, &C. for Their Religion, and All This by Military Force, by Order of the Executive* (Detroit: Dawson and Bates, Printers, 1839), 35; also in Johnson, *Mormon Redress Petitions*, 79.

20 Charles C. Rich, "Extract from Charles C. Rich's History," *Latter-day Saints' Millennial Star* 26, no. 28 (July 9, 1864): 441; and Rich, Petition, in Johnson, *Mormon Redress Petitions*, 707.

21 Lilburn W. Boggs to John B. Clark, October 27, 1838, in *Document*, 61. For a more extensive examination of the Battle of Crooked River, see Baugh, "The Battle between Mormon and Missouri Militia at Crooked River," in *A Call to Arms*, 99–113.

22 Reburn I. Holcombe [Burr Joyce], "The Haun's Mill Massacre: An Incident of the 'Mormon War' in Missouri," *St. Louis Globe-Democrat*, October 6, 1887, n.p.; also published in Joseph Smith III and Heman C. Smith, *The History of the Reorganized Church of Jesus Christ of Latter-Day Saints*, 4 vols. (Independence: Herald House, 1951), 2:227.

23 Ellis Ames, Reminiscence, *Journal History of the Church*, October 30, 1838, 14, Church History Library. Ames is incorrectly identified in the *Journal History* as Ellis Eamut.

24 For a more extensive examination of the Hawn's Mill Massacre, see Baugh, "The Massacre at Haun's [Hawn's] Mill," in *A Call to Arms*, 115–34; also Alexander L. Baugh, "Jacob Hawn and the Hawn's Mill Massacre: Missouri Millwright and Oregon Pioneer," *Mormon Historical Studies* 11, no. 1 (Spring 2010), 1–25. For an analysis of the massacre in connection with the extermination order, see Alexander L. Baugh, "The Haun's [Hawn's] Mill Massacre and the Extermination Order of Missouri Governor Lilburn W. Boggs," *Mormon Historical Studies* 10, no. 1 (Spring 2009), 21–30.

25 Ebenezer Robinson, "Items of Personal History of the Editor," *The Return* 2, no. 1 (January 1890), 206.

26 John Corrill, *A Brief History of the Church of Jesus Christ of Latter-day Saints (Commonly Called Mormons), Including an Account of Their Doctrine and Discipline; with Reasons of the Author for Leaving the Church* (St. Louis: For the Author, 1839), 42.

27 Lyman Wight, Petition, in Johnson, *Mormon Redress Petitions*, 660; also in *History of the Church*, 3:445. For a more extensive examination of the Mormon defense of Far West, see Baugh, "The Mormon Defense of Far West," in *A Call to Arms*, 135–147.

28 For a more extensive examination of the Mormon surrender, militia occupation, and Richmond hearing, see Baugh, "Surrender and Military Occupation," in *A Call to Arms*, 149–170; see also Alexander L. Baugh, "'Silence, Ye Fiends of the Infernal Pit': Joseph Smith's Incarceration in Richmond, Missouri, November 1838," *Mormon Historical Studies* 13, nos. 1–2 (Spring/Fall 2012), 135–159.

29 Hyrum Smith, Affidavit, in Clark, *Mormon Redress Petitions*, 636; also Hyrum Smith, "Testimony of Hyrum Smith," *History of the Church*, 3:421. The Mormon prisoners later testified that "by order of the Governor of the State of Missouri, [they] were set at large, with directions to leave the State without delay." Caleb Baldwin, et al., Affidavit, in Johnson, *Mormon Redress Petitions*, 684–685. Hyrum Smith, Caleb Baldwin, Alexander McRae, and Lyman Wight's names appear on the affidavit, but Joseph Smith's does not.

30 For an account of the release of the Liberty Jail prisoners by the Missouri authorities, see Alexander L. Baugh, "'We Took Our Change of Venue to the State of Illinois': The Gallatin Hearing and the Escape of Joseph Smith and the Mormon Prisoners from Missouri, 1939," *Mormon Historical Studies* 2, no. 1 (Spring 2001), 59–82.

31 For a historical analysis of the Mormon prisoners incarcerated in Richmond Jail, see Alexander L. Baugh, "The Final Episode of Mormonism in Missouri in the 1830s: The Incarceration of the Mormon Prisoners in Richmond and Columbia Jails, 1838–1839," *John Whitmer Historical Association Journal* 28 (2008), 1–34; and Alexander L. Baugh, "'Tis Not for Crimes That I Have Done': Parley P. Pratt's Missouri Imprisonment, 1838–1839," in *Parley P. Pratt and the Making of Mormonism*, ed. Gregory Armstrong, Matthew J. Grow, and Dennis J. Siler (Norman, OK: Arthur H. Clark Company, 2011), 137–167.

32 Lilburn W. Boggs to the House of Representatives of the State of Missouri, December 5, 1838, in *Document*, 14; also in *Missouri Republican* (St. Louis, MO), December 10, 1838.

33 See "Exterminate," in Noah Webster, *Noah Webster's First Edition of an American Dictionary of the English Language* (New York: S. Converse, 1828), n. p.

34 Christopher S. Bond, Executive Order, June 25, 1976, Missouri State Archives, Jefferson City, Missouri. Interestingly, members belonging to the LDS Church assumed Bond issued his rescindment with the Utah Church specifically in mind when in fact he issued the announcement to a group of RLDS (now Community of Christ) Far West Stake members at Stewartsville, Missouri. See Richard P. Howard, "Time and Reconciliation," *Saints' Herald* 123 (October 1976), 36.

Alexander L. Baugh (alex_baugh@byu.edu) is a professor in the Department of Church History and Doctrine at BYU. He received his BS from Utah State University and his MA and PhD degrees from Brigham Young University. He specializes in researching and writing about the Missouri period of early LDS Church history (1831–1839). He is currently the editor of *Mormon Historical Studies*, co-director of research for the Religious Studies Center at BYU, and a volume editor for the *Joseph Smith Papers*.

## CHAPTER FOUR

# BARBAROUSLY EXPELLED

## The Infamous Nauvoo War of September 1846

### RICHARD BENNETT

It is with much satisfaction that I am enabled to state, that the people called Mormons have been removed from the state. The great body of them removed voluntarily, but a small remnant of them were barbarously expelled with force, and in a manner which reflects but little credit on the state or its institutions.[1]

So announced Governor Thomas Ford before the general assembly of the state of Illinois in December 1846. Ford spoke with a forked tongue—as relieved as he was by the departure of the hated Mormon people from Nauvoo, their "City Beautiful," he was ashamed by the illegal and brutal manner by which they were driven out. He could speak of "satisfaction" only in the sense that no further county war had erupted. It was a sordid resolution to a highly complex, powder-keg situation.

Even though it was not the notorious extermination order of his Missouri counterpart, Lilburn W. Boggs, eight years previously, the resultant sufferings resulting from the Battle of Nauvoo amounted to the same. What happened in Nauvoo in September 1846 remains one of the most despicable events in both Mormon and Illinois history.

Forty-five-year-old Thomas Ford, a Democrat, served as governor of Illinois when the Latter-day Saints were expelled from the state in 1846. He was also the chief executive who promised the Prophet Joseph Smith the protection of the state when Joseph and Hyrum were murdered at Carthage Jail in June 1844.

## THE POOR CAMPS

The truth is the unofficial count of those killed in the Battle of Nauvoo is three, all on the Mormon side.[2] However, many others in the subsequent so-called "Poor Camps"

The Latter-day Saints began their exodus to the Rocky Mountains in February 1846—in the heart of a Midwest winter. This premature departure came in part as a result of threats of a military force coming against the Saints at Nauvoo.

of hundreds of Mormon refugees eventually perished in the winter of 1846–1847, victims of having been driven out of their homes and into the teeth of unforgiving winter without adequate food and provisions. From all accounts, both Mormon and otherwise, their state was a pitiful one. Scores of families crossed the Mississippi River into Iowa to flee mob action. From there some went up the river to Burlington or Galena, while others went down the river to St. Louis or other places. Most followed in the wake of the earlier companies as they crossed Iowa. While returning to Washington after his successful intermediary efforts at raising the Mormon Battalion near Council Bluffs, Thomas L. Kane stumbled upon these Poor Camps and penned the following scene of suffering:

> Dreadful indeed, was the suffering of these forsaken beings. Cowed and cramped by cold and sunburn, alternating as each weary day and night dragged on, they were, almost all of them, the crippled victims of disease. They were there because they had no homes, nor hospital nor poor-house nor friends to offer them any. They could not satisfy the feeble cravings of their sick: they had not bread to quiet the fractious hunger cries of their children. Mothers and babes, daughters and grand-parents, all of them alike, were bivouacked in tatters, wanting even covering to comfort those whom the sick shiver of fever was searching to the marrow.[3]

Mason Brayman, a special emissary sent by Governor Thomas Ford to survey the realities of the post-battle situation, provided this blunt and highly critical assessment:

> Bands of armed men traversed the city, entering the houses of citizens, robbing them of arms, throwing their household goods out of doors, insulting them, and threatening their lives. Many were seized, and marched to the camp, and after a military examination set across the river for the crime of sympathizing with the Mormons, or the still more heinous offense of fighting in defense of the city under the command of officers commissioned by you and instructed to make that defense. It is, indeed, painfully true that many citizens of this state have been driven from it by an armed force, because impelled by our encouragement and a sense of duty, they have bravely defended their homes . . . from the assaults of a force assembled for unlawful purposes.[4]

One struggling, faithful Mormon widow, Elizabeth Gilbert, who like many others sensed rightly the coming storm, begged for help from Brigham Young, who then was leading the Saints some three hundred miles west at the Missouri River:

> It [Nauvoo] is truly a lonesome and dismal place. . . . I want to know what I shall do[.] Is it best for me to remain among the gentiles? . . . My body is almost worn out a struggling to get a shelter for my head. . . . Tell all my friends that I yet live and my faith in the gospel is as firm as the everlasting hills and strangism [the teachings of James Strang] has no effect on my mind. . . . If you think it wisdom for me to come out this fall how shall I gather[?] Council me as though I was your child or Sister and whatever you say that I will do.[5]

Thomas L. Kane was called the "friend of the Mormons," and rightly so. His heart was touched by scenes of the Saints huddled and suffering on the banks of the Mississippi River across from Nauvoo. He would write appeals on behalf of the Saints that touched many in the East.

## THE BATTLE OF NAUVOO

The 1846 Battle of Nauvoo was but the lengthened shadow of violence that had terminated in the deaths of the Mormon Prophet,

Joseph Smith, and his brother, Hyrum, in Carthage Jail two years earlier. Their murder was the harbinger of even worse things to come, and Brigham Young knew it. The enemies of the Church would not be content until every last Mormon was out of their state. One resolution after another had made such sentiments dastardly clear—they either leave on their own or be forcibly driven out. There would be no compromise.

By the fall of 1845, local mob vigilantes were busy harassing outlying Mormon farms and small settlements, easy prey for their crimes. On November 15, a considerable party set fire to a stack of straw near Solomon Hancock's barn near Green Plains and concealed themselves. While attempting to put out the fire, Hancock was fired upon by the intruders; his friend, In Edmund Durfee, was shot and killed on the spot.[6]

Such bloodshed led the Mormons to step up their own military maneuvers. Amid preparations for their exodus to the West, several marched, mustered, paraded, and devised plans for defending the city against a possible attack. Such activities continued on after the first vanguard companies of Latter-day Saints had crossed the Mississippi River on February 4, 1846, in what would become a wholesale Mormon exodus to the West. Some 2,500 Mormons were already across the river by March 15, and many thousands more would come in the months that followed.[7] By September, fewer than one thousand remained in the city. The Mormon intent was clearly obvious: to quit the state just soon as possible, although not everyone could afford to leave that quickly.

Although the charter authorizing the Nauvoo Legion as an arm of the Illinois state militia had been repealed in January 1845, the Legion continued to function as a police force of the Church to protect its members.[8] Its remaining members who were left behind were given two primary functions—to protect those crossing the river and to ensure the safety of as many of those temporarily remaining behind as possible. It was the Legion that ensured the safety of those involved in the Nauvoo Temple dedication ceremonies in April and May 1846. By mid-August, according to one informal census, only "250 males old and young" with accompanying wives and children remained in the city. As Porter Rockwell aptly described it, "Nauvoo is getting to be a very mean place."[9]

According to historian Glen M. Leonard, who has written perhaps the most comprehensive study on the topic, the Battle of Nauvoo really began in June 1846 when a group called the Convention of Hancock County Old Citizens convened at Carthage, the county seat, to plan Independence Day festivities.[10] Several of the very same men who had spearheaded the mob martyrdom of Joseph Smith two years earlier—including Thomas C. Sharp, editor of the nearby *Warsaw Signal*, and Levi Williams—and who had recently been exonerated of the charge of murdering Joseph Smith, now boldly decided that Hancock County could not celebrate independence as long as their enemies still lived in the county.[11] Once again taking the law into their own hands, and though well aware that the Mormons were leaving the state, several hundred armed volunteers led by Williams marched toward Nauvoo to demand its immediate surrender and evacuation.

CARTHAGE.

Thomas Sharp, newspaperman and enemy to the Saints, was the catalyst that caused the martyrdom of Joseph and Hyrum Smith. Not satisfied, he would rally the enemies of the Church again in 1845–1846 to drive the Saints from the state once and for all.

Governor Ford, likewise convinced that the Mormons were moving west, had earlier withdrawn Major William B. Warren, a Whig clerk of the Illinois Supreme Court, from Nauvoo along with his small contingent of ten state militiamen. Satisfied that all the Mormons would adhere to Brigham Young's declaration that they be out of the city by mid-summer, Warren had also warned the anti-Mormon factions not to plan military action against the city. To do so would violate a previously-issued order prohibiting

Ads from the *Hancock County Eagle*. The Saints had to leave Hancock County, thus requiring that they sell their houses for whatever price they could get.

more than four armed men from assembling unless they were state troops.[12]

However, not all the Mormons had followed Brigham Young's counsel. Some sided with the "new citizens" of Nauvoo, non-Mormons who had recently purchased vacated Mormon homes. Others were unprepared to leave. The fact is, the city could not empty itself soon enough of its former inhabitants and was an irritation to the impatient forces gathering in Carthage. Declared Sharp in an attempt at further agitation, "There is no peace for Hancock while a Mormon remains in it."[13] In hindsight, Warren's departure was premature.

Upon hearing the news of an invading party, Colonel Stephen Markham and Hancock County Sheriff Jacob Backenstos hastily organized a "ragtag" Nauvoo militia made up of Mormon defenders in concert with several new citizens. Sensing a larger armed force of defenders than they had anticipated, the Hancock County vigilantes—or "Regulators," as they called themselves—forestalled their frontal attack plans in favor of quarantining the city, forbidding any access or egress except by ferry to Iowa.

Throughout a hot July, with both tempers and temperatures rising, more armed men from around the county heeded Sharp's call and flocked to Carthage, where they began scattered preparatory military maneuvers. More than that, they captured, whipped, and held hostage several Mormons who had ventured outside of the city to work as farmhands. Sharp's declaration of war left Hancock County farmers in a state of uneasiness bordering on panic, so much so that their crops went unharvested.

Major Warren and other reliable state militia officers had been recently recruited to fight in the Mexican War—so when word of these events reached Springfield, Governor Ford dispatched Major James R. Parker of the 32nd Regiment of the Illinois State Militia with a token force of ten militiamen from nearby Fulton County to Carthage with the full authority of the state "to keep the peace."[14] Parker, a Democrat, was ill received. John Carlin, special constable of Hancock County and a leading Whig, with now more than one thousand armed men at his disposal, flatly rejected Parker's authority. When attempts to ensure peace were roundly rebuffed, Parker, seeing he was vastly outnumbered, backed off. Colonel Thomas S. Brockman, a Campbellite preacher, now took command of the growing Carthage militia.

Increasingly fearful for Nauvoo's safety, yet unwilling to call out more units of the state militia to prevent a county war, Governor Ford tried diplomacy one more time by asking two leading citizens of nearby Quincy, Illinois, for assistance. Quincy, be it remembered, had ever treated the Mormons with fairness, humanitarianism,

As the mobs approached the city, the Nauvoo Temple bell sounded the alarm. When the city fell, the non-Mormons proclaimed their victory from the temple's tower.

and compassion. Back in 1839, as the Mormons were hounded out of Missouri, it was the citizens of Quincy who, like Good Samaritans, had taken the Mormons into their homes, befriended them, and offered them protection. Unlike Warsaw and other anti-Mormon river towns, Quincy had continued in its tradition of fairness and open-mindedness toward the Latter-day Saints. Hence it should come as no surprise that Governor Ford turned to Quincy at this impasse.

He first appointed Major Benjamin Clifford of Quincy (who also owned land and a store in Nauvoo) to replace the discredited Parker as head of the state forces in the city. Second, he commissioned the highly respected John M. Wood, long-time mayor of Quincy, to do all in his power to negotiate a truce. Responding to the governor's request, Wood hurried to Nauvoo, reaching the city on September 10. Wood reached Nauvoo not a minute too soon: on that same day, Brockman was marching his Carthaginians toward the Mormon capital. Wood immediately sent orders to the approaching force to disband, but his pleas fell on deaf ears.

With Brockman's forces now on the march, the Nauvoo Temple bell sounded the alarm. That evening, Brockman set up camp at Hunter's Farm, just east of the city. Throughout the night some 250 men and boys in Nauvoo hastily erected breastworks, planted land mines on incoming roads, fitted out four makeshift cannons built from old, discarded steamboat chimney shafts, and otherwise prepared to give battle. Meanwhile, many of the women and children clustered together in homes and shelters near the temple while others, including Emma Smith, the Prophet's widow, and her five children defied the quarantine and fled the city for Fulton, Illinois, to join relatives and such Mormon dissenters as William Marks. Lucy Mack Smith, mother of Joseph Smith, had already fled to Knoxville, Illinois.

Clifford had placed most of his forces ten blocks east of the Nauvoo Temple near Winchester Street, between Knight and Mulholland streets. He was now ably supported by Mormon leaders John S. Fullmer (one of the Nauvoo Trustees), William Cutler, and Daniel H. Wells, who organized the defenders into three companies under the command of Captain Hiram Gates, Captain William Anderson, and Captain Andrew Lamoreaux.

Friday morning saw Brockman attempting to encircle the defenders by coming down La Harpe Road. Some thirty sharpshooters under Captain Anderson—soon called "the Spartan Band"—rushed northwestwardly from upper Parley Street to engage the invaders. As Leonard notes, the two forces engaged in long-range fire, perhaps a distance of fifty yards, "the Spartans with their repeating rifles, the invaders with cannon."[15] There were no casualties on either side in this first skirmish. Rapidly running short of ammunition, Anderson, a former captain in the Nauvoo Legion, fired his steamboat cannon,

Daniel H. Wells lived in the area that would become Nauvoo before the Saints arrived. He became their friend and ally and was baptized in August 1846. As hostilities erupted in Nauvoo, Daniel Wells was among the city's defenders. He would later become a member of the First Presidency and a counselor to President Brigham Young.

often with spent cannon balls that had already been fired by the Regulators.[16]

Saturday, September 12, turned out to be the bloodiest and most decisive day in the battle. After the defenders refused to unconditionally surrender, the Regulators, fresh with new ammunition and supplies, prepared for an all-out frontal attack, with Mayor Wood and others watching

at a distance from the temple tower.[17] With the support of six cannons, Brockman marched his five hundred men on the city "in excellent order, under the most skillful military discipline," swinging south to avoid the breastworks.[18] Fighting broke out from house to house and from street to street, with both sides firing on each other with deadly earnest.

Almon W. Babbitt, Esq., another of Nauvoo's trustees, had his horse shot from under him. For reasons not clear, William Anderson and his Spartan Band, including Jesse and Alexander Molen, suddenly moved from beyond the protection of the buildings, jumped the fence, and boldly faced the advancing forces. Within seconds, in what was the deciding turning point, Anderson was shot in the breast by a musket ball. His dying words were, "I am wounded; take my gun and shoot on."[19] Immediately after, his fifteen-year-old son, Augustus Anderson, was also killed. Another Mormon defender, David Norris, the father of five children, soon lay mortally wounded on the ground, virtually decapitated by a cannon ball. Another half dozen defenders were soon wounded, including Benjamin Whitehead, John E. Campbell, Curtis E. Bolton, and Hiram Kimball. Several of the attackers were also wounded, many seriously, although apparently none was killed. In the meantime, Daniel H. Wells, a Nauvoo justice of the peace, and Andrew L. Lamoreaux led a short-lived, spirited counterattack with little result.

Soon thereafter, Wells prevailed upon his fellow defenders, some of whom wanted to continue fighting, with these stern words of counsel concerning his own beloved Nauvoo: "What interests have the Saints to expect from its defense? Our interests are not identified with it, but in getting away from it. Who would urge the propriety of exposing life to defend a place for the purpose of vacating it?"[20] By

unstained - such officer a affairs to be under a pledge
to use no violence, if not resisted.

3. The Mormons to deliver up their arms
to persons to be mutually agreed on by the con-
tending parties - If said parties cannot agree,
then this committee to receive the arms; to be
redelivered to the proper owner, or persons appointed by the Mormons to receive them, when
they shall have left the State.

4. A committee of not more than
five persons, with their families, if they have
them to be appointed by the Mormons, to arrange
their affairs in Nauvoo- and reside there, if
necessary, till the first of May next.

5. This committee to appoint Ten men
to reside in or near Nauvoo, to see the treaty
enforced; and Genl Brockman, or any officer
appointed by him, to remain in camp with a
force not exceeding 200 men, the committee
of Ten to have free access to the City and to
the Camp, and make daily reports to the officer
commanding, who shall pledge himself that
neither life nor property be destroyed in Nauvoo.

It is proper to advise you that the suspension
of hostilities was agreed to, on the part of Genl.

This treaty between the warring factions in Nauvoo was signed on September 16, 1846, and marked the end of the Battle of Nauvoo. It gave possession of Nauvoo to the mob from Carthage.

late Saturday, now short of ammunition and men and recognizing the futility of further resistance and the inevitability of more bloodshed, the defenders hoisted a white flag of surrender, an initiative that was at first rebuffed by their enemies. By this time, a disgusted Mayor Wood had quit the city only to be replaced by other men of the "Quincy Committee of One Hundred" led by Andrew Johnson, who hastily crafted terms of surrender—"The Articles of Accommodation, Treaty and Agreement." This treaty, signed on September 16, officially ended the fighting. [21]

Since to the victor go the spoils, the terms of peace were mere articles of capitulation—an imposition more than a negotiation—and were decidedly in favor of the Carthaginians. Nauvoo would immediately surrender its forces and arms; the occupation forces would enter the city at 3 P.M. the very next day but pledged to protect Nauvoo citizenry and property from any further harm; the sick, women, and children would be treated "with humanity"; all remaining Mormons must leave the city "as soon as they could" (in other words, within ten days); the Nauvoo Trustees, including Fullmer, Babbitt, and Heywood, would be allowed to remain behind with their clerks to sell off Church and private properties; and the key to the temple must be surrendered to the negotiating committee. On Wednesday afternoon, the invaders entered Nauvoo.

While they killed no one who remained in the city, the victors were not slow in breaking their pledge. In true mob action, they seized many local citizens, forced them from their homes, and threw several into the river, where they performed mock baptisms. They burned fields, broke open trunks and chests, and desecrated the temple. A mob preacher wasted no time in ascending to the top of the temple tower and, standing outside, proclaimed in a loud voice, "Peace, Peace, Peace to all the inhabitants of the earth, now the Mormons are driven." [22] Such was the ending of the Battle of Nauvoo and the beginning of the Poor Camps alluded to earlier. Soon the conquered city lay desolate and deserted, a forlorn memory of happier days.

## CONCLUSION

In conclusion, we must ask the following questions. First, was military action against Nauvoo sanctioned by the state—in other words, was it militia or mob activity? From the evidence presented herein, it is obvious that Brockman and Carlin rebuffed every state overture at peace and went against the orders of the chief executive of the state. At the same time, however, Governor Ford showed no interest in sending a sufficiently large number of Illinois militiamen to put an end to the fighting. It was a case of a feigned rebuke by the state and a forced invasion by mob vigilantes. Governor Ford was not complicit in the attacks but did little of substance to prevent them. He wanted as quick an end to the Mormon problem as possible with the least amount of bloodshed.

Second, did Mormon leadership expect such hostilities and sanction military defensive action? Certainly Brigham Young and the Quorum of the Twelve did not expect a full-scale attack, especially not when the Mormons showed clear intent to leave. "I have never believed the Lord would suffer a general massacre of this people by a mob," he wrote from western Iowa. "If ten thousand men were to come against us, and no other way was open for our deliverance, the earth would swallow them up." [23]

The Poor Camps experienced the "miracle of the quail" and other tender mercies that preserved their lives until they could be rescued by their fellow Saints, who had been sent back from Winter Quarters to retrieve them.

Clearly Brigham Young had expected the city to be entirely vacant by the end of the summer as a result of his specific earlier orders. He had seen the writing on the wall a year earlier and had put into action a full-scale plan of exodus. Part of that plan was covenant-based, in that all covenanted before they left Nauvoo to bring as many others as possible. As Brigham Young said in late September 1846 to those who were being sent back to eastern Iowa to help bring out the stranded refugees: "Let the fire of the covenant which you made in the House of the Lord, burn in your hearts, like flame unquenchable, till

The Saints were gone from Nauvoo by autumn 1846, leaving the city desolate and its temple a silent sentinel and reminder of the former glory of the "City Beautiful."

you, by yourselves or delegates, have searched out every man . . . and bring a load of the poor from Nauvoo."[24]

To fight with vastly inferior numbers against a growing foe would have been the height of foppery to a pragmatic leader like Brigham Young. As Wells put it, "Who would urge the propriety of exposing life to defend a place for the purpose of vacating it?" The decision to use armed force to defend the city was therefore a local one, hastily made and perhaps unwise, considering the odds. Nevertheless, it was arguably defensible considering the lawless intent of the invading force.

Third, was the Nauvoo Legion officially involved? The answer is certainly no, since most members of this now-unchartered unit were on their way west.

Finally, what was the heritage of the Battle of Nauvoo? It must be said that the Carthage forces acted with the same blind venom that they had shown in the earlier martyrdom of Joseph Smith. They resisted state authority, knowing full well that a weak governor would not interfere. Theirs was a legacy of lawlessness, although they showed fine military prowess on the battlefield. On the other hand, the defenders showed enormous courage against overwhelming numbers to fight as they did. Their efforts at holding off a far superior force is a legacy of sacrifice, but how well spent? In the end it was an unnecessary, illegal, deplorable activity that led to the expulsion of hundreds of Mormon refugees, some of whom would perish in the snows of Iowa and Nebraska in large measure because of the unjust cruelties they had suffered in Nauvoo.

Today the city of Nauvoo stands as a witness to a yesterday full of faith and hurt, with little memory or record of any battle or bloodstains. Perhaps that is as it should be.

# Endnotes

1   *Monmouth Atlas,* 18 December 1846. As cited in Richard E. Bennett, Susan Easton Black, and Donald Q. Cannon, *The Nauvoo Legion in Illinois: A History of the Mormon Militia, 1841–1846* (Norman, OK: The Arthur H. Clark Company, 2010), 261.

2   The numbers of those killed in the attacking force has never been determined; however, several accounts tell of many wounded with the strong likelihood that some also died.

3   Thomas L. Kane, *"The Mormons." A Discourse Delivered Before the Historical Society of Pennsylvania, March 16, 1850* (Philadelphia: King and Baird Printers, 1850), 9–10.

4   Robert Lang Campbell, Diary, September 21, 1846, 42, L. Tom Perry Special Collections, Harold B. Lee Library, Brigham Young University, Provo, Utah. Brayman Report, September 18, 1846. See also B. H. Roberts, *A Comprehensive History of The Church of Jesus Christ of Latter-day Saints* (Provo, UT: Brigham Young University Press, 1965), 3:17–18.

5   Elizabeth Gilbert to Brigham Young, 13 August 1846. Brigham Young Papers. LDS Church Historical Library, Salt Lake City, Utah. For a much more thorough study of the Mormon Poor Camps, see the author's "'Dadda, I Wish We Were Out of This Country': The Nauvoo Poor Camps in Iowa, Fall 1846," a paper delivered at the Iowa Mormon Trails History Symposium, Des Moines, Iowa, May 3, 1996, and published in *The Iowa Mormon Trail—Legacy of Faith and Courage,* Susan Easton Black and William G. Hartley, eds. (Orem, UT: Helix Publishing, 1997), 155–170.

6   *History of The Church of Jesus Christ of Latter-day Saints,* 7 vols. (Salt Lake City: Deseret Book Company, 1973), 7:523. See also William G. Hartley, *The 1845 Burning of Morley's Settlement and Murder of Edmund Durfee* (Salt Lake City: Primer Publications, 1997).

7   William Hartley, "Spring Exodus from Nauvoo: Act Two in the 1846 Mormon Exodus Drama." in *The Iowa Mormon Trail,* Susan Easton Black and William G. Hartley, eds. (Orem, UT: Helix Publishers, 1997), 61–83.

8   Richard E. Bennett, Susan Easton Black, and Donald Q. Cannon, *The Nauvoo Legion in Illinois: A History of the Mormon Militia, 1841–1846* (Norman, OK: The Arthur H. Clark Company, 2010), 252–256.

9   Diary of Heber C. Kimball, 20 August 1846, LDS Church Historical Library.

10  Glen M. Leonard, *Nauvoo: A Place of Peace, A People of Promise* (Salt Lake City: Deseret Book Company; and Provo, UT: Brigham Young University Press, 2002), 600–621.

11  Dallin H. Oaks and Marvin S. Hill, *Carthage Conspiracy: The Trial of the Accused Assassins of Joseph Smith* (Urbana, IL: University of Illinois Press, 1979), 113–190. Sharp, Williams, and others had been acquitted of the charge of conspiracy in the death of Joseph Smith the year before.

12  Leonard, *Nauvoo,* 597.

13  Leonard, *Nauvoo,* 602.

14  From the transcript of the "Account of the Battle of Nauvoo," by John S. Fullmer. On file at the Nauvoo Land and Records Office, Nauvoo, Illinois.

15  Leonard, *Nauvoo,* 609.

16  From the Louisa Lyman Nielsen and Dora Dutson Family History. Nauvoo Land and Records Office.

17  See "Sketch of the Nauvoo Battle" as found in the "John S. Fuller Account," Nauvoo Land and Records Office.

18  Fullmer, "Account of the Battle." One Mormon woman counted 72 cannon shots. See Louisa (Norris) Decker, "Reminiscences of Nauvoo," *Woman's Exponent* 37 (March 1909): 41–42, 49–50.

19  Andrew Jenson, "Battle of Nauvoo," *Historical Record,* June 1889, 853.

20  Journal of Wandle Mace, Special Collections, BYU, 100–102.

21  The Articles of Accommodation were signed by John S. Fullmer, Joseph L. Heywood, Almon W. Babbitt, Andrew Johnson, Thomas S. Brockman, and John Carlin.

22  Thomas Bullock to Franklin D. Richards, *Millennial Star,* 10 (January 15, 1848). As cited in Leonard, *Nauvoo,* 614.

23  From comments in a speech given by Brigham Young at Winter Quarters, 27 September 1846, *Journal History of the Church,* LDS Church Historical Library.

24  Brigham Young to the High Council at Council Point, 28 December 1846, *Journal History of the Church,* LDS Church Historical Library.

# CHAPTER FIVE

# THE UTAH WAR (1857—1858)

## "A dark time for the Saints"

### KENNETH L. ALFORD

> With us, it is the kingdom of God, or nothing; and we will
> maintain it, or die in trying—though we shall not die in trying.
> —Brigham Young, 18 October 1857[1]

Observers attending Fourth of July celebrations across Utah Territory in 1857 would have been hard-pressed to find any evidence that the Mormon celebrants were anything but loyal Americans. In Ogden, the Constitution of the United States was read during a public meeting in the tabernacle. In Kaysville, Pleasant Grove, and elsewhere, roasts were offered throughout the day on behalf of President Buchanan, the Constitution, and the government of the United States. Across the territory, celebrating Saints unfurled and saluted the American flag. Yet at the same time, thousands of American soldiers were marching on Salt Lake City in what would soon become known as the Utah War.[2] This essay provides an overview of the war and how it affected the Latter-day Saints.[3]

## BACKGROUND

In 1847, there was a strong sense among Mormons that they had finally found a place they could settle in peace. Safely established in the Rocky Mountains, many Latter-day Saints felt they were now beyond the reach of serious persecution, but Utahns and federal territorial officials experienced a rocky relationship in the 1850s.[4] Federal appointees sent negative reports to Washington several years before the Utah War; the anti-Mormon reports of territorial associate justice W. W. Drummond were among the worst. There was clearly little love lost between Utahns and some of the political appointees who served in the territory. Brigham Young characterized many

President Brigham Young declared the valley of the Great Salt Lake as "the right place." It was to become the place from which the ensign prophesied by Isaiah was raised and where the Saints were to gather—their place of safety and refuge.

political appointees to Utah as "damned, rotten-hearted scoundrels" and "poor, miserable blacklegs, broken-down political hacks, robbers, and whoremongers."[5] In July 1857 the *Deseret News* acknowledged that "lying letters, though written by nobodies, have excited and bewildered the public mind."[6]

Following the election of President James Buchanan, calls for military intervention in Utah became increasingly louder as Eastern newspaper headlines warned of "Mormon Outrages" and "Mormon Rebellion" while advocating "War with the Mormons."[7] In April 1857, the *New York Times* reported that the Mormons had "200,000 spies and agents scattered throughout the country . . . [and they are] in close alliance with 300,000 Indians upon our Western border."[8] Amazing claims—especially considering that in 1857 there were only 55,236 Mormons in the entire world and a sizable number lived in Great Britain.[9]

Appointed by US President James Buchanan to serve in Utah Territory, Perry E. Brocchus was among those territorial officials who came to Utah for a time and returned to the East embittered and spreading malicious rumors about the Saints. Those rumors contributed to a federal army marching on Utah.

Mormonism was reportedly a "social ulcer" that "had assumed so malignant a form that longer forbearance of the knife is not to be tolerated" lest it "seriously compromise the character and endanger the tranquility of the country."[10] Individual Mormons were "semi-savage," "steeped in mystery and sunken in mental powers," and "an active, enterprising people, [who] are all the more closely to be watched on that account."[11] Some writers believed Mormons were guilty of "murders, arsons, robberies, and the forcible debauch of defenseless women."[12] Harsh living conditions in Utah Territory—described by one Eastern reporter as "comfortless, and so far from inviting or favoring the commonest decency in living, actually forbid it, by rendering it impossible. Squalid poverty stares at us from every door and window. Not one woman in ten has a pair of shoes to her feet, their garments are of the coarsest material, and their children [are] ragged, half naked, shockingly dirty, and rude as young Indians"—were viewed as indicative of the debased nature of Mormons.[13]

President Buchanan did not mention Utah during his inaugural address on 4 March 1857, but within a few weeks he became convinced that Utah was in rebellion. On 28 May 1857 soldiers were ordered to march on Utah. The military force bound for Utah is often popularly called "Johnston's Army"—named after Col. (later brevet brigadier) Albert Sidney Johnston (who, while serving as a senior Confederate general during the Civil War, would later give his life in 1862 during the battle of Shiloh).

William S. Harney, an Indian fighter widely known by the nicknames "Squaw Killer" and "Mad Bear," was initially selected to lead the army to Utah.[14] Alerted by General Winfield Scott on 28 May that he was "likely to command" the Utah Expedition, Harney did not receive official instructions until early July—orders that proclaimed Utah "in a state of substantial rebellion."[15] Harney remained in Kansas, though. Exactly how Johnston replaced Harney in command has remained a mystery; at the time of his selection, Johnston was a regimental commander fighting Indians in Texas with his executive officer, Lt. Col. Robert E. Lee.[16]

As historian and noted Utah War authority William P. MacKinnon has written, exactly when Brigham Young first learned of the army's march on Utah "is complicated and shrouded in Mormon mythology as well as federal fumbling."[17] Young may have learned of the military expedition as early as 29 May during dinner with Apostle George A. Smith, who heard rumors in St. Louis of a two- to three-thousand-man force bound for Utah, or he could have received the news from Abraham Smoot, Orrin Porter Rockwell, and Judson Stoddard, who arrived in Salt Lake City on 22 or 23 July.[18] If not, then Brigham Young most certainly learned on 24 July when Smoot, Rockwell, and Stoddard dramatically interrupted tenth anniversary Pioneer Day celebrations at Silver Lake in Big Cottonwood Canyon[19] as "the stars and stripes were unfurled on two of the highest peaks in sight of the camp"— vividly fulfilling Brigham's July 1847 request, "If the United States will now let this people alone for ten years to come, we will ask no odds of them or any one else but God."[20] Sadly, as Brigham noted, the ten-year peace enjoyed in Utah from 1847 to 1857 was "the longest rest that the Saints have ever had at one time."[21] Regardless of when Brigham Young learned of the army's approach, the key point to note is that he learned indirectly and not through official notification from the president of the United States to the serving governor of Utah Territory.

Two days later, on 26 July, President Heber C. Kimball, a counselor in the Church's First Presidency who had "been driven five times" from previous homes, offered his view that the army would "take brother Brigham Young and Heber C. Kimball

### The Salt Lake Infamy—What Should Be Done.

In addition to still later intelligence from Utah received by last night's mail, we publish this morning a letter from Judge Drummond, late of that Territory, which fully corroborates the tale of Mormon wrong and oppression presented in our Salt Lake correspondence. The startling facts detailed in these communications can hardly fail to take deep hold upon public sentiment, and through it reach the heart and nerve the hands of the National Administration to speedy and decisive action. Already the tide begins to swell towards Washington, bearing upon its bosom a stern demand for needed succor to our fellow-citizens now writhing beneath the heel of Mormon theocracy; and we cannot but hope, despite Judge Drummond's gloomy forebodings, that Mr. Buchanan will give immediate and practical attention to this subject in preference to the distribution of foreign spoils.

There is much truthful satire in the suggestion of a cotemporary that the surest method of securing Mormon subjugation is to send a dozen runaway negroes into the Territory, who will of necessity draw a regiment of troops

Eastern newspapers printed articles trumpeting perceived iniquities of the Latter-day Saints in the West. These articles were little grounded in fact and often assailed the sensibilities of Easterners, leading to concerted calls that "something must be done about Utah."

Officially designated the Utah Expedition, the army marching on Utah left too late in the year to make it to Salt Lake City.

and others, and they will slay us . . . they will put us under martial law and massacre this people." He then expressed his feelings regarding federal officials who had slandered the Saints: "Drummond and those miserable scoundrels . . . how do I feel towards them?—pray for them? Yes, I pray that God Almighty would send them to hell." He then famously declared, "Send 2500 troops here . . . God Almighty helping me, I will fight until there is not a drop of blood in my veins. Good God! I have wives enough to whip out the United States, for they will whip themselves."[22]

## THE ARMY'S UTAH EXPEDITION

The deployment of troops to Utah Territory in 1857–1858 was formally designated by the federal government as the Utah Expedition.[23] A popular pioneer adage predicted that companies on the plains who reached Independence Rock, in present-day Wyoming, before the 4th of July would find safe passage to Salt Lake City before winter snows began. The Utah Expedition did not leave Fort Leavenworth, Kansas, until late July—a decision they would soon regret.

One of the army's first actions was to send Captain Stewart Van Vliet, US Quartermaster, and an advance party to Salt Lake City in an attempt to purchase supplies for the approaching army. Brigham Young graciously hosted Van Vliet and invited him to sit on the stand during 13 September 1857 meetings in the Bowery.[24] With Van Vliet sitting nearby, Brigham announced, "They say that their army is legal, and I say that such a statement is as false as hell, and that they are as rotten as an old pumpkin that has been frozen seven times and then melted in a harvest sun."[25] He further declared that if the army forced its way into the valley, "they would find nothing but a barren waste. We should burn every thing that was wood and every acre of grass that would burn . . . They will not find any thing to eat in this Territory when they come."[26] Elder John Taylor spoke next. Near the end of his sermon he asked, "All you that are willing to set fire to your property and lay it in ashes, rather than submit to their military rule and oppression, manifest it by raising your hands." The *Deseret News* reported that "the congregation unanimously raised their hands."[27] Van Vliet dutifully reported the meeting's events to his superiors.

After leaving Fort Leavenworth, Kansas, in July, the army moved ponderously across the plains toward Utah. Capt. Jesse A. Gove, of the Tenth US Infantry, remarked that their supply train alone was nine miles long and took six companies to guard it.[28]

## UTAH'S RESPONSE

In August, Church leaders dispatched Apostle George A. Smith—for whom St. George, Utah, is named—to Southern Utah with letters of instructions and guidance. A possible connection between this direction and the Mountain Meadow Massacre that occurred the following month, on 11 September 1857, has been vigorously debated by historians.[29]

On 15 September, shortly after Van Vliet's departure, Brigham Young—acting as territorial governor—issued a proclamation placing Utah on a war-time footing. Announcing that "We are invaded by a hostile force," the Proclamation forbid "all armed forces, of every description from coming into this Territory, under any pretense whatsoever," placed the territorial militia "in readiness to march, at a moment's notice" to repel the invasion, and declared martial law throughout the Territory.[30]

Brigham Young explained that "if it should become a duty to take the sword, let us do it, manfully and in the strength of Israel's

Captain Stewart Van Vliet, a US Army quartermaster officer, was sent to Utah in advance of the Utah Expedition to purchase food and supplies from the very people the army was coming to confront. Latter-day Saint leaders treated him graciously but declined his request.

The intentions of the army coming to Utah were unclear. Hence, President Brigham Young declared martial law across Utah Territory in September 1857 and encouraged citizens to be prepared.

Opposite Bottom: As part of the preparations for the coming of Johnston's Army, General Daniel H. Wells, commander of the Nauvoo Legion and counselor to Brigham Young in the Church's First Presidency, ordered territorial militia men into Echo Canyon, where they built breastworks and fortifications—remnants of which are still visible today.

God."[31] The Nauvoo Legion, under the command of General Daniel H. Wells[32] (who also served as Brigham Young's second counselor in the Church's First Presidency), began preparing Echo Canyon to resist a possible armed invasion. Hundreds of militia members built breastworks, dug trenches, built dams, and loosened rocks in case they should be needed as weapons.

The Latter-day Saint's military strategy can be extrapolated from General Wells's fall 1857 instructions to Nauvoo Legion Maj. Joseph Taylor to "take no life" and to Col. William H. Dame to "save life always if it is possible—we do not wish to shed one drop of blood if it can be avoided."[33] Militia members were ordered, though, to "annoy them in every possible way," and to "use every exertion to stampede their animals and set fire to their trains. Burn, the whole country before them, and on their flanks."[34] Mormons are credited with destroying seventy-four government supply wagons (carrying an estimated 300,000 pounds of food and supplies) as well as capturing 1,400 head of cattle.[35] Henry Hamilton, who served as a young soldier in the Utah Expedition, noted that the "Mormons, now began to trouble us considerably. . . . Every day when coming to camp they would set the grass on fire, using long torches, and riding swift horses, so that before pitching tents, we always had to fight fire."[36]

The most famous incident associated with harassing the army occurred near Green River during the night of 4–5 October. As Lot Smith, who as a sixteen-year-old was the youngest member of the Mormon Battalion, was preparing to burn wagon master John M. Dawson's supply train, Dawson said, "For God's sake, don't burn the trains." Smith later reported, "I said it was for His sake that I was going to burn them."[37]

Brigham Young explained that "Lot was a terror to that whole army, they would rather see the devil than see him," but he asked, "Was anybody hurt? No." Young also quoted Col. Edmund Alexander, the expedition's acting commander prior to Johnston's arrival, as commenting that the "Mormons were wonderfully annoying. . . . You cannot look on a hill but you may see Mormons, or down into a valley but there is Mormons, if you try to get out of sight a little there's Mormons, what the devil does it mean they are everywhere!'"[38]

In February 1858, President Young announced that militia soldiers "are required to go just as a man goes on a preaching mission. A man that does not go with his heart right before God we do not want him to go at all," and he promised those "who go in a right way will never be overtaken by an enemy, they won't be caught asleep, [and] their horses will not be taken from them."[39]

The mail contract for the Brigham Young Express and Carrying Company (often referred to as the Y. X. Company), organized in 1856, was revoked in July 1857 at the beginning of the war.[40] The cancellation of the Y. X. Company's mail contract hit the Church particularly hard. Nearly $200,000 had been spent during the previous winter building way stations, hiring employees, as well as purchasing equipment, teams, and wagons. Church resources "were almost exhausted in this venture." To help finance the costs associated with the war, the Church created the Deseret Currency Association, which issued $66,936 in two series of a new currency called "Deseret script."[41]

The Latter-day Saints were instructed not to shed blood but to delay the coming of the army. Nauvoo Legion soldiers, such as Lot Smith (above) and Orrin Porter Rockwell, rode onto the plains of Wyoming and burned the prairie, set fire to supply trains, and drove off the army's stock animals.

## THE WINTER OF 1857–1858

Referring to the Mormon handcart companies of the previous year, the *New York Times* feared that the army might fare

Bottom: *Echo Canyon* © Dennis Lyman

worse on the plains than homesteaders and Mormon converts. "The [Mormon] emigration of last season, four-fifths of which consisted of women and children, started out in August, and made the entire trip on foot, hauling their bedding and provisions in hand-carts. If Uncle Sam's war men can't compete with women and children in their marches, and in ability to take care of themselves in a new and rude country, with all their advantages, appointments and ample means of transportation, surely they deserve the finger of scorn pointed at their puerile effeminacy."[42]

Army plans called for the Utah Expedition to reach the Salt Lake Valley prior to winter. Mormon harassment and internal delays combined to force the army into winter quarters near Fort Bridger. The Mormons burned Fort Bridger and neighboring Fort Supply prior to the army's arrival, and the army spent a difficult winter at nearby Camp Scott.[43] Large numbers of livestock died due to the extreme conditions; accommodations were crude, food was scarce, and the army ran out of salt (sardonically, just one hundred miles from the Great Salt Lake).

In December 1857, more than six months after he ordered federal troops to march to Utah, President Buchanan finally broke his public silence on the Utah Expedition. During his first annual message to Congress, he noted that "the present condition of the Territory of Utah, when contrasted with what it was one year ago, is a subject for congratulation. It was then in a state of rebellion, and cost what it might, the character of the Government required that this rebellion should be suppressed and the Mormons compelled to yield obedience to the Constitution and the laws."[44]

The delays caused by their late start and by harassment from Mormon raiders forced the Utah Expedition to winter near Fort Bridger, Wyoming, which was then part of Utah Territory.

Much of the Congressional debate regarding the Utah Expedition would sound familiar today: the mission was unclear and the cost was too high. Then, as now, Congressional representatives complained that there were "no backward tracks when our Government began to spend money."[45] During Congressional debate, it was suggested that the cost of the Utah Expedition could have "paid the expenses of our entire ocean mail service for years" or purchased a trans-

continental railroad.[46] By April 1858, there was "an increasing disposition in Congress to check further movements of the Utah Expedition."[47] When President Buchanan sent his budget message to Congress in June 1858, it was reportedly met with loud laughter on the floor of the House of Representatives.[48]

# PLENTIFUL MISUNDERSTANDINGS

Mormons and the Utah Expedition captured the popular imagination and were the focus of many news stories during 1857–1858—second in frequency only to slavery and the Kansas Territory.[49] Mormons were considered devious foes who had prepared, it was claimed, all manner of devilish defenses to stop the army from entering the Salt Lake Valley.

Many of the rumors reported by newspapers told of army massacres at the hands of the Mormons. General William S. Harney—who never actually marched with the army—supposedly lost 600 men to Mormon marauders in October 1857.[50] Colonel Albert Sidney Johnston reportedly lost 160 soldiers in December 1857 and an additional 180 men in January 1858 as well as "all the provisions, mules and horses."[51] A "horrible rumor" from January 1858 related the fallacious story of 200 men in Lieutenant Colonel Philip St. George Cooke's command being butchered, "a number taken prisoners, and all the officers hung."[52] According to reports printed in May 1858, both Captain Anderson and the Mormon militia who reportedly attacked him lost three-fourths of their soldiers.[53] Colonel Johnston supposedly lost another 250 soldiers in May 1858, and afterwards the Mormons were said to have driven his army "before them for a distance of 150 miles."[54]

Yet all of those reports were false. A January 1858 *New York Times* article noted that a "little common sense bestowed upon the Mormon question would not be out of place just now. Our people have been carried away by reports of massacres, murders and treason, and in their horror at these outrages, which have

The US Capitol Building— By the spring of 1858, there was growing discontent within Congress regarding the Utah War. Some Congressmen felt that the transcontinental railroad or other worthy projects could have been completed for what was spent on the Utah Expedition.

been contradicted as often as not, they have not paused to investigate their truth."[55]

## THE MOVE SOUTH

From the earliest months of the Utah War, Brigham Young threatened to execute a Sebastopol strategy. Sebastopol, a city on the Black Sea, figured prominently during the Crimean War. British, French, and Ottoman forces, commanded by Lord Raglan, laid siege to the city of Sebastopol for more than a year (1854–1855). When it became apparent to Sebastopol's Russian defenders that the city would be lost, they burned the entire city rather than surrender it to their enemies.[56]

In a 16 August 1857 discourse, Brigham Young declared, "If they come here, and it is necessary I will tell you what I shall do. I shall lay this building in ashes, I shall lay my dwelling house in ashes, I shall lay my mills in ashes, I shall cut every shrub and tree in the Valley, every pole, every inch of board, and put it all into ashes. I will burn the grass, and the stubble and lay it waste . . . I will take this people in the midst of these mountains. . . ."[57]

A War Council—consisting of the First Presidency, eight Apostles, and thirty militia officers—was held in the Church historian's office on 18 March. After discussion and speeches, President Young announced it was his plan "to go into the desert and not war" with the army.[58] Three days later, during Sunday special conference meetings held in the Tabernacle, it was resolved "to move all the people [from the northern settlements] and provision[s] to the southern country and go into the desert as soon as possible and evacuate this city and be ready to burn the whole city to [the] ground before our enemies come to take possession of it."[59]

The Siege of Sebastopol clearly made a significant impact on Brigham Young, and he made several direct references to Sebastopol during the 21 March conference: "I am for letting them [the army] come and take 'Sebastopol [sic],'" "they may have 'Sebastopol' after it is vacated, but they cannot have it before," and "get ready, so that when the army comes in here we can swing our hats and say, you are welcome to Sebastopol."[60]

Articles such as this example from the May 5, 1858, edition of the *New York Times* grossly exaggerated the war in Utah and often portrayed the Latter-day Saints as butchers.

## LATEST BY TELEGRAPH.

### From St. Louis.

RUMORED SKIRMISH WITH THE MORMONS—ARRIVAL OF ARMY OFFICERS—FREE-STATE NOMINATIONS IN KANSAS.

ST. LOUIS, Tuesday, May 4.

The Leavenworth *Ledger* says that a dispatch from Utah reached the Fort on Monday last, asking for a reinforcement, and giving an account of a skirmish between a guerilla party of Mormons and a body of troops under Capt. ANDERSON, in which three-fourths of the combatants were killed on both sides. A company of light and heavy artillery, and a company of dragoons were immediately dispatched from the Fort. The statement is discredited here.

The Leavenworth *Herald*, of the 1st, tells the story as follows: "News reached the Fort by Express that a band of outlaws and a small detachment of troops under Capt. ANDERSON, had an engagement in the Little Osage country, that one soldier was killed and that Capt. ANDERSON was wounded in the leg, and had his horse killed under him. A battery of four guns and a company of dragoons were dispatched to the scene of the difficulty." The statement from the Leavenworth *Ledger*, already telegraphed, grew out of the above, probably by the substitution of Camp Scott for Fort Scott.

The following officers of the United States Army have arrived here: Gen. Smith, Gen. Harney, Col. Johnson, Major Maera, Major Chapman, Captain Humphreys and Captain Pleasanton.

The Free-State Convention to nominate State officers, met at Topeka, Kansas, on the 28th ult. H. J.

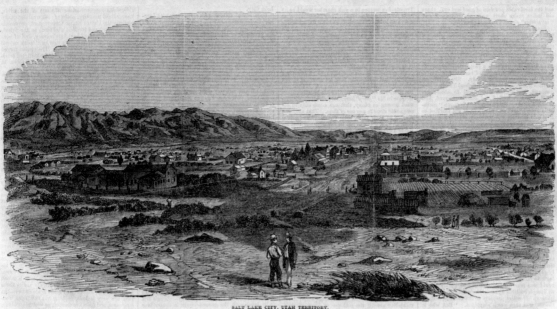

SALT LAKE CITY, UTAH TERRITORY.

In the morning Tabernacle conference session on 21 March, President Young said the Saints should "leave before we are obliged to." Asking the congregation, "Where are you going [to go]?," he answered, "To the deserts and the mountains. There is a desert region in this Territory larger than any of the Eastern States, that no white man knows anything about. . . . Probably there is room in that region for 500,000 persons to live scattered about where there is good grass and water. I am going there, where we should have gone six or seven years ago. Now we are going to see whether the sheep will follow the shepherd." Interestingly and uncharacteristically, this was one of the few instances in which Brigham Young openly expressed doubt regarding his actions. He confided to the Saints, "Do not come to my office to ask me whether I am mistaken, for I want to tell you now perhaps I am."[61]

The "Move South," as the evacuation was soon named, began in earnest as the first families began "packing up for leaving." A few days later the worst snowfall of the winter exacted a terrible toll on the settlers who were moving south. By the first week of April, General Conference weekend, Wilford Woodruff reported that "the roads are lined with men, women and children, teams and wagons all moving south."[62]

The exodus was actually quite orderly considering the scope and circumstances. Church congregations north of Utah County were assigned a provisional destination in Utah, Juab, Millard, or Iron counties.[63] Under the direction of local bishops, many wards organized into companies with captains—similar to the organization used to cross the plains.[64] Soon the main road that

Salt Lake City circa 1858— Known as the "Sebastopol policy"—named after a year-long siege of the Russian city of Sebastopol during the 1853–1856 Crimean War—President Brigham Young announced that he would burn Salt Lake City to the ground if the United States Army tried to forcibly occupy it.

Johnston's Army was coming, and even as it descended through Echo Canyon approaching Salt Lake City, some 30,000 Latter-day Saints left their homes and fled south in accordance with President Brigham Young's counsel.

tied all of the major settlements together was reportedly jammed for fifty miles with people and wagons. The population in and around Provo in Utah County ballooned from four thousand to twelve or fifteen thousand.[65] Lorin Farr, one of Ogden's founding fathers, observed that "accommodations of the crudest kind were all that Provo could offer."[66] Wilford Woodruff reported, "Many suffered and some came near perishing. Horses died by the wayside. Men unloaded their goods in the mud. Others took their team off and left their wagons sticking in the mud. Some teams gave out and whole families lay in the mud under their wagons overnight. Women carried their children in their arms and waded in water mud and snow knee deep."[67] Northern communities often moved in several stages—stopping briefly in Ogden and then in Salt Lake City before heading farther south.[68]

Construction work on the Salt Lake Temple stopped immediately. Less than a week after the announcement of the Move South, workers hid stone cut for the temple and plowed "up around the Temple foundation to cover it with dirt."[69] Tabernacle window casings and heavy equipment were also buried. The Tabernacle organ and many wagonloads of Church property were moved south.[70] From May to September 1858, the *Deseret News* was published in Fillmore, Utah (which served as Utah's territorial capital from 1851–1856).

A letter later printed in the *Millennial Star* reported on the Move South, "Go where you will, you will see the Saints making cheerful preparations for their departure, and a word of comfort on their lips for their neighbors; notwithstanding which, a keen observer might perceive a glistening in the eye of some of the stoutest among us. We have enough to eat, and for that we are thankful."[71] All dislocated families did not fare as well. Joseph C. Kingsley, who lived near Ogden, moved his family to Provo "with considerable trouble." His wife, Dorcas, "was not well all the time." He found it difficult "to earn anything by my hands," and his family was continually "in want of clothing." After "peace was made . . . [when we] had the privilege of moving back if we choose," he moved his family to Salt Lake City.[72]

As word of the Move South reached the East, the country became convinced that Brigham Young would take his followers and leave Utah Territory. Speculation ran wild. Press reports throughout 1857–1858 claimed the Mormons were planning to relocate to a number of different destinations. At one time or another, Mexico, British territories, Russian territories, Oregon, Vancouver, Washington Territory, the Sandwich Islands, "northern regions," the "Feejees or Fidjis [*sic*] Islands," the White River Mountains, the Marquesas, the Samoan islands, lower California, New Guinea, Nicaragua, Oceanica, and Cedar City in southern Utah Territory were all identified as sites for a possible Mormon relocation.[73]

A January 1858 *New York Times* report noted that rumors about the Saints leaving Utah may have even influenced the army's 1858 summer campaign plans—"all accounts concur

The Salt Lake Temple circa 1858—Not wanting the temple block to be desecrated, workers buried the foundation and stones of the temple, leaving the temple block resembling a plowed field.

## The Future Home of the Mormons.

"What is to be done with the Mormons?" is becoming a question of general interest. If in so brief a time they have become so formidable to the Government that an increase of the Army, and an additional cost of our military preparations to the extent of some ten millions of dollars annually, are required to keep them in subjection, what will they require some ten or twenty years hence, when their numbers will be doubled, and their insolence will have undergone a proportionate increase? It must begin to dawn upon the minds of the Mormons themselves that they cannot live any longer, quietly and securely, in the heart of a Christian country. They must either conquer or be conquered, or else remove to some remote island beyond the jurisdiction of any Christian Government, for it is impossible that such a community should exist under any Government that is based on Christian principles. There is no room for these fanatical people either on this Continent or those of the Old World. There is no secure spot for them to pitch their tents in, except among some of those groups of islands in the South Pacific

"The Future Home of the Mormons," *New York Times*, February 10, 1858—Speculation ran rampant in the East that the Latter-day Saints would abandon the Rocky Mountains and move elsewhere. Newspapers enjoyed speculating where the Saints might relocate—Mexico, Canada, and even Fiji were suggested as possible destinations for the Saints.

in saying that the Mormons will leave Utah Territory in the spring, and it is said that Col. Johnston is so firmly of this belief that he asks no increase of the numerical force of the army under his command."[74] John M. Bernhisel, the Congressional delegate from Utah Territory, announced "positively, that the Mormons are not leaving Salt Lake Valley," but to no avail.[75] Rumors continued even after the war's end.

The exact number of Latter-day Saints who participated in the Move South is unknown—with 30,000 being a conservative estimate.[76] As historian Clifford L. Stott noted in *Search for Sanctuary,* the "Saints who were rapidly emptying Salt Lake City had no place to settle!"[77] Therefore, shortly after "the Move South" was announced, Brigham Young sent an expedition, under the direction of George W. Bean, a one-armed adventurer and explorer from Provo, to find "a place suitable to stop."[78] A few weeks later, Young called William H. Dame, a stake president in Parowan, to lead a second expedition into the western desert to search for a new home for the Saints.[79] The two expeditions traveled more than 2,000 miles searching in vain for a habitable resettlement location.

Most of the people displaced by the Move South settled temporarily in Provo and points farther south. Lorenzo S. Clark, though just six years old at the time, later recorded memories of his family's living conditions in Spanish Fork. He wrote, "Our dug-out was about 14 or possibly 16 feet square, and near four feet deep. The middle was built up with gable ends, so the center was three or four feet higher than the sides. Either three or four large poles were laid from gable to gable with willows crosswise of the poles. Weeds were placed over the willows and dirt on top of them. . . . If there was a door to close, I have forgotten it."[80]

The feelings associated with abandoning their homes must have been intense. Mary Ann Young, one of the prophet's wives, represented many Latter-day Saints when she said, "I am in favor of leaving here without fighting. I am very comfortably situated, but I would be sorry to think that one good brother's life was lost in defending my home. I would rather leave peaceably. . . . God will bless us . . . and we shall be happy on the desert."[81] Brigham Young arrived in Provo "with 22 wagons and part of his family and their household goods" on 30 April and moved into "a number of shanties."[82] Andrew Jackson Allen, a Nauvoo Legion soldier who moved his family to Utah County from Salt Lake City, "set them down" in Utah County "without any covering, only a wagon cover on a wagon box"; yet he felt confident enough in Brigham Young's leadership that he declared the "present move south" was "the salvation of this people."[83]

When Governor Alfred Cumming visited "Toille [Tooele] City" at the end of April, "he found all the people moving. He said my God have I come too late to stop all this moving and burning of property?" But the Move South continued and must have presented quite a scene—"North to the South the road is lined for 50 to 100 miles from Box Elder to Provo with horse, mule & ox teams and loose cattle, sheep & hogs and also men women & children. All are leaving their homes."[84] In mid-May, Governor Cumming implored Brigham Young to persuade "those who respect your opinion, and who are moving south, that there is no ground for the apprehension, which they appear to entertain."[85] A census taken in Salt Lake City on 27 May 1858 listed only 2,450 residents left in Salt Lake—one thousand of whom were in the process of moving south from northern parts of the territory.[86] Robert T. Burton, who later served in the Church's Presiding Bishopric, summed up the Move South when he confided to his journal, "We have homes but no home."[87]

Occasionally, sympathetic news articles appeared in the States. One article from June 1858 commented on the Move South. "Whatever our opinions may be of Mormon morals or Mormon manners, there can be no question that this voluntary and even cheerful abandonment by 40,000 people of homes created by wonderful industry in the midst of trackless wastes, after years of hardship and persecution, is something, from which no one who has a particle of sympathy with pluck, fortitude and constancy, can withhold his admiration." The reporter observed that "right or wrong, sincerity thus attested is not a thing to be sneered at. True or false, a faith to which so many men and women prove their

Brigham's Shanties— During the Move South, many of those who were displaced from their homes in northern Utah settled in Provo, where they built shanty towns.

BRIGHAM'S SHANTIES AT PROVO CITY.—[FROM A PHOTOGRAPH BY BEER & MOSS.]

"The Mormon Exodus," *New York Times*, 17 June 1858—Referring to the Mormons' Move South earlier that spring, a June 17, 1858, editorial in the *New York Times* declared that "right or wrong, sincerity thus attested is not a thing to be sneered at. True or false, a faith to which so many men and women prove their loyalty by such sacrifices, is a force in the world."

loyalty by such sacrifices, is a force in the world."[88]

# FINDING A PEACEFUL SOLUTION

On Christmas Day 1857, Thomas L. Kane, a non-Mormon but longtime friend of Brigham Young and the Latter-day Saints, met with President Buchanan in the White House and volunteered his service as a negotiator to bring the Utah War to a peaceful conclusion. Kane was "determined to go [to Utah Territory], whether with his [Buchanan's] approbation or not."[89] Buchanan approved Kane's trip and his efforts to resolve the Utah War, but at Kane's insistence the president did not make Kane an official government representative.[90] Kane traveled to Utah via Panama and California.

Wilford Woodruff recorded that on 25 February 1858 Thomas L. Kane, who "was very pale and worn down having travelled night and day," met with Church leaders in Salt Lake. After discussing the situation of the Saints, Kane called upon their "sympathies in behalf of the poor soldiers who are now suffering in the cold and snows of the mountains and request you to render them aid and comfort and to assist them to come here and to bid them a hearty welcome into your hospitable valley."[91] Referring to Kane's haggard physical appearance, Brigham Young reportedly said, "Brother Thomas the Lord sent you here and he will not let you die. No you cannot die until your work is done."[92]

In early April, Thomas L. Kane and Governor Alfred Cumming passed through Echo Canyon at night on their way to Salt Lake City. Utah militiamen formed two lines and presented arms as the governor passed; Cumming remarked that they were fine soldiers.[93] On 15 April, Governor Cumming notified General Johnston that "I have been everywhere recognized as Governor of Utah . . . [and] universally greeted with such respectful attentions as are due to the representative authority of the United States in the Territory."[94]

In addition to Thomas L. Kane serving as an unofficial negotiator, President Buchanan also authorized two official government negotiators—Lazarus W. Powell, a senator-elect and ex-governor of Kentucky, and Benjamin McCulloch, a Texas Ranger and future Confederate general who rejected Buchanan's offer in May 1857 to serve as Utah's governor—to visit Utah and obtain a peaceful conclusion to the tense situation.[95] On 11 June 1858, the Church's First Presidency, Quorum of the Twelve, and other leaders met with the peace commissioners in the Council House. Wilford Woodruff recorded that "President Buchanan sent by them a proclamation accusing us of treason and some 50 other crimes all of which was false yet he pardoned us for all those offenses if we would be subject to the Constitution and laws of the United States and if we would let his troops winter in our Territory."[96] Regarding the presidential pardon, Brigham Young commented: "It is true that Lot Smith burned some wagons containing government supplies for the army. This was an overt act, and if it is for this that we are to be pardoned, I accept the pardon."[97] A peaceful solution was reached, and Young consented to the army marching through the valley on condition that they would not stop within the city.

Flags flew at half-staff as the army marched through Salt Lake City on 26 June 1858.[98] Elizabeth Cumming, Governor Cumming's wife and secretary, wrote to her sister-in-law that "the army passed

through [Salt Lake City] in excellent order. Tired, & dusty & hot, yet not a man nor a mule stepped out of place."[99] Captain Randolph B. Marcy of the Fifth Infantry stated: "We marched through the city with colors flying and bands playing, but, to our astonishment, we only saw here and there a very few persons. The city seemed to have been deserted."[100] George William McCune, a Mormon militiaman, explained, "There were about 500 of us hid in the houses along South Temple Street, with loaded rifles and our orders 'to let them have it' if they interfered with anything; then we were to set fire to the houses, and flee to the mountains. But the government troops were very orderly and marched through very quietly."[101] A newspaper correspondent described the army's entry into Salt Lake: "All day long from dawn until sunset, the troops and trains poured through the city, the utter silence of the streets being broken only by the music of the

The Utah Expedition marched through Salt Lake City on June 26, 1858, under strict orders not to break formation. Latter-day Saints were standing by, out of view, with orders to burn the city if the army attempted to take possession of it. Dutifully, the army passed through and made camp on the west side of the valley.

military bands, the monotonous tramp of the regiments, and the rattle of the baggage wagons. . . . The stillness was so profound that during the interval between the passage of the columns, the monotonous gurgle of City Creek struck every ear."[102]

Speaking in Provo the following day, Brigham Young promised that as "soon as General Johnston finds a place to locate his command . . . we will go home. . . . It will not be long." Shortly thereafter, the army established Camp Floyd on the west side of Utah Lake, and the Saints began to return to their homes.

## THE WAR'S COST

Asa S. Hawley, a soldier in the Nauvoo Legion, observed that the "feeling amongst our people at that time was truly intense."[103] Another Utah resident categorized the Utah War as "a dark time for the saints."[104] Reminiscing in 1869, Utah pioneer Jean Rio Griffiths Baker wrote that the "famine of the year '57 and the move South in '58 are matters of history, and I need only say that I passed through both and a bitter experience it was."[105]

Speaking about the Utah War, Brigham Young rhetorically asked the nation, "Have you counted the cost?"[106] The war is sometimes portrayed as a bloodless conflict with no lingering affects, but that simplistic view is mistaken. Hundreds of lives were lost during the conflict (most tragically at Mountain Meadows). The war interrupted tens of thousands of lives throughout the territory and also affected The Church of Jesus Christ of Latter-day Saints, Utah Territory, and the nation.

Most Utahns lived a hardscrabble existence and could ill afford the

Colonel Albert Sidney Johnston established Camp Floyd thirty miles from Salt Lake City on the west side of Utah Lake. The army would remain garrisoned there until shortly after the outbreak of the Civil War.

economic costs that accompanied the war. This was especially true for families who were dislocated during the Move South. Militia military assignments removed fathers from families. Crops were not planted, livestock died, schools were closed, and wartime inflation squeezed many settler budgets to the breaking point.

For nineteenth-century Latter-day Saint leadership, managing a growing worldwide organization before the arrival of the telegraph and railroads was challenging enough, but doing so from the middle of Utah Territory increased the challenge under the best of circumstances. The Utah War made Church administration even more difficult. Work on the Salt Lake Temple ceased. Missionary work and new Church publications slowed to a trickle. Church meetings were cancelled for several months. Tithes and offerings went uncollected. The "Tabernacle was closed, no public meetings were held, and the members of the First Presidency retired and were seldom seen. Heber and others routinely provided an armed escort for President Young when it was necessary for him to appear in public."[107] And the Church's Relief Society, only recently reorganized, was suspended.

The war fundamentally changed Utah Territory. Plans for new settlements were abandoned or delayed. The growth of many existing settlements was hampered as settlers were called to return to Salt Lake City. On 5 September 1857, for example, 450 Saints loaded 123 wagons and began a two-month journey from Carson Valley (in present-day Nevada) to Salt Lake City—arriving on 2 November.[108] Postal communication, a continuing trial to early Western settlers, was seriously interrupted by the war. Immigration slowed between 1858 through 1860—a lagging effect of the war.[109] Demographic changes initiated by the Utah War affected the Saints profoundly. As Brigham Young succinctly observed before the army's arrival, "You might as well tell me that you can make hell into a powder-house as to tell me that you could let an army in here and have peace."[110] In northern Utah, violence, prostitution, and drunkenness increased.[111] Life in Utah never returned to the pre-war status quo.

The Utah War cast Utah and the Mormons onto a national stage like never before, and the view most Americans held was distinctly negative. Utahns and Mormons—inextricably linked in the public mind—were principally viewed as disloyal and un-American. In 1858, the *New York Times* reported that the "general feeling of the people of the Union in all sections, and of all sects and parties, is so decidedly adverse to the Mormons, that the Government is not

The old tabernacle in Salt Lake City was closed during much of the Utah War. Public meetings of worship were canceled, missionary work came to a halt, and other effects of the war hindered the work of the Church. The Utah War was conducted at great cost to the nation and the Church.

likely to be held to a very strict account for its acts towards them, even though they should be utterly exterminated, or driven from their present resting-place."[112] That distrust played out in multiple ways for more than half a century following the Utah War. For example, shortly after the Civil War ended in 1865, the *New York Times* suggested that "in the Spring of 1861 South Carolina was more loyal to the Union than Utah is today."[113]

The Utah War also affected the nation. Following the war, both Congress (in 1858) and the presidency (in 1860) changed hands from Democratic to Republican control. When the Civil War began in 1861, the largest Union troop concentration was in Utah Territory—more than one thousand miles from where the soldiers were needed. The Utah War provided both Northern and Southern armies with significant military leadership and experience. It also left the United States treasury depleted—a cause of great concern to the newly inaugurated Lincoln administration.[114] In hindsight, the nation recognized that the millions of dollars spent to prosecute the Utah War and sustain the army in the aftermath could have been better spent.

## SUMMARY

An editorial in the *Deseret News* on 2 June 1858 noted that "a more striking contrast cannot well be imagined than that now presented before the whole country by the administration of the two territories, Utah and Kansas." President Buchanan, the writer noted, had declared Kansas "in a state of rebellion," and even though Kansas "may rebel, convulse the Union from centre to circumference, be the means of producing sectional feuds of the most dangerous and bloody character and diffuse an influence throughout the Republic that seriously threatens to result in civil war," the president's solution was Kansas's "speedy admission . . . as a sovereign state!" While at the same time, Utah, "who possesses equal claims on the Federal Government and the magnanimity of its officers, is decried as traitorous and every engine of oppression put in operation to humble her."[115]

Shortly before the army entered the Salt Lake Valley, the *New York Times* mocked President Buchanan's policy by noting that "the Prophet, has not turned out as well as expected, and refuses to be a traitor."[116] Buchanan was the brunt of criticism from both sides of the conflict. As early as September 1857, Brigham Young observed: "I think that James Buchanan has got in a bad fix."[117] Apostle George A. Smith summarized Buchanan's situation by saying, "The Republican organs whipped Mr. Buchanan into the Utah war, and they then whipped him for getting into it; and they whipped him until he got out of it the best way he could, and then they whipped him awfully for getting out."[118]

The same week that Johnston and the Utah Expedition marched into the Salt Lake Valley, the *New York Times* published their editorial conclusions regarding the Utah War: "The Mormon war has been unquestionably a mass of blunders from beginning to end. It was begun without knowing whether the Mormons would submit without fighting or not. The troops were then set in motion in Autumn when they ought to have been set in motion in Spring. When they had suffered horribly, and lost their baggage-train in the snow, peace commissioners were thought of, and negotiations set on foot." Governor Cumming, the editorial continued, "was to have entered as a conqueror; he entered in perfect peace and quietness. He wrote home that all was right—General Johnston wrote home that all was wrong. He said he was *de facto* as well as *de jure* Governor of Utah—Johnston said he was a prisoner." The bottom line for the *Times* was that "whichever way we look at it, it is a great

**Light Wanted on the Mormon Difficulty.**

We are very glad to learn that a resolution was adopted yesterday in Congress, on the motion of Mr. ZOLLICOFFER, of Tennessee, calling on the President for information in relation to the difficulty with the Mormons, as to the causes for the Utah Expedition, and whether BRIGHAM YOUNG is actually in a state of rebellion or resistance to the United States authorities. The resolution will probably elicit some highly interesting information, and furnish the people with satisfactory reasons for the extraordinary preparations which appear to be on foot for sending a great military force to Salt Lake City. We have had an abundance of reports of Mormon outrages, and we are bound to believe that there are satisfactory reasons for the military expedition to Utah; but all the information that has been given to the public has been of a rather vague character, and much of it has come through channels which justify a suspicion that it has been considerably exaggerated. What the public desire to know, and have a right to demand, is an official statement of the actual facts of the

In an article dated January 28, 1858, the *New York Times* voiced the sentiments of many in the United States when it blamed the Latter-day Saints for the Utah War and called for their extermination.

In a *New York Times* article on June 23, 1858, the Utah War was broadly summarized as "a great mass of stupid blunders." By its conclusion, the war was unpopular with both sides.

mass of stupid blunders."[119] An article printed the previous week was just as blunt: "An army was sent to chastise rebels, before it was clearly ascertained whether or not there were any rebels to chastise."[120]

The Utah War was perhaps summarized best by *New York Herald* special correspondent Lemuel Fillmore's published report on 19 July 1858 when he stated it "may thus be summarily historized: killed, none; wounded, none; fooled, everybody."[121] Writing several years later, George Cannon Lambert, who lived in Utah during the war, reflected that "To make a show of resistance for the moral effect it would have was one thing, but to come in actual conflict with the army of the United States was quite another thing. The Church leaders had time for sober second thought, and wisdom prevailed."[122]

Given the high degree of political tensions and emotions involved, the Utah War ended as amicably as possible. John Jaques, who later served as an assistant Church historian, summed up the frustration and waste associated with the Utah War when he penned the following lines in his poem "The Mormon Question":

Buchanan had avoided

Much guilt and keen remorse,

If he'd not sent to Utah

The cart before the horse.[123]

When Thomas L. Kane departed Utah in early May 1858 to return home, he carried a letter from Brigham Young addressed to missionaries returning to Utah. After offering advice on which trails to take in order to avoid Indians and mountaineers, Brigham ended his letter optimistically by noting, "The Lord is at the helm of the old ship 'Zion,' and she sails well."[124] Throughout the war there remained a quiet confidence among most Latter-day Saints that God was in control.

# Endnotes

1. Brigham Young, Remarks in Salt Lake City Tabernacle, 18 October 1857, in *The Complete Discourses of Brigham Young,* 5 vols., ed. Richard S. Van Wagoner (Salt Lake City: The Smith-Petit Foundation, 2009), 3:1357. Spelling standardized.

2. Salt Lake City was called Great Salt Lake City until an official name change in 1868. This essay will use the more familiar name.

3. To learn more about the Utah War, see, for example, William P. MacKinnon, ed., *At Sword's Point, Part I: A Documentary History of the Utah War to 1858,* vol. 10, *Kingdom in the West: The Mormons and the American Frontier* (Norman, OK: The Arthur H. Clark Company, 2008); MacKinnnon's *At Sword's Point, Part II* is forthcoming; Leroy Hafen, *Utah Expedition, 1857–1858: A Documentary Account* (Norman, OK: The Arthur H. Clark Company, 1983); David L. Bigler and Will Bagley, *The Mormon Rebellion: America's First Civil War 1857–1858* (Norman, OK: University of Oklahoma Press, 2011); as well as numerous books and journal articles.

4. Utah Territory was created on 9 September 1850 as part of the Compromise of 1850.

5. Brigham Young, Remarks in Salt Lake City, 13 September 1857 and 28 February 1858, in *The Complete Discourses of Brigham Young,* 3:1338, 1410.

6. "A Fair Proposal and a Few Plain Truths," *Deseret News,* July 29, 1857.

7. "War with the Mormons," *New York Daily Times,* 13 May 1857; "The Mormon Outrages," *New York Daily Times,* 1 May 1857; "The Mormon Rebellion," *New York Daily Times,* 11 May 1857; and "Preparations in Utah for Resisting Federal Authority," *New York Daily Times,* 1 May 1857.

8. "News of the Day," *New York Daily Times,* 21 April 1857.

9. "Church Statistics," [LDS] *2012 Church Almanac* (Salt Lake City: Deseret News, 2012), 203.

10. "What Shall We Do with the Mormons?," *New York Daily Times,* 21 April 1857; "A Patriot Wanted," *New York Daily Times,* 29 May 1857.

11. "Utah and the Mormons," *New York Times,* 15 May 1858; "Interesting from Utah," *New York Times,* 23 August 1858; "The Governorship of Utah, *New York Daily Times,* 30 March 1857. (The *New York Daily Times* dropped the word "Daily" and became the *New York Times* on Monday, 14 September 1857.)

12. "The Salt Lake Infamy—What Should Be Done," *New York Daily Times,* 20 May 1857.

13. "One Week Later from Utah," *New York Times,* 13 August 1858.

14. As historian William MacKinnon noted, "by the time of the Utah War, the army had court-martialed him [Harney] four times and a civil court

had tried (but acquitted) him a fifth time for bludgeoning a defenseless female slave to death." MacKinnon, *At Sword's Point, Part 1,* 168.

15. MacKinnon, *At Sword's Point, Part 1,* 169–171.

16. MacKinnon, *At Sword's Point, Part 1,* 378.

17. MacKinnon, *At Sword's Point, Part 1,* 223.

18. The trio, who were accompanied back to Salt Lake City by Parley P. Pratt's widow, Elinor McLean Pratt, also brought news of Parley P. Pratt's assassination on 13 May in Van Buren, Arkansas, and informed Brigham Young that the Y. X. Company's mail contract had been cancelled. See MacKinnon, *At Sword's Point, Part 1,* 224.

19. As historian Eugene E. Campbell explained, "[Brigham] Young had invited some 2,500 people to join him for a three- or four-day anniversary celebration. People had begun wending their way to the mouth of Big Cottonwood Canyon on 22 July, and the next morning Young led a long line of carriages and wagons into the canyon. Before noon the cavalcade had reached the campground at Silver Lake some 8,000 feet above sea level. Early in the afternoon the company camped, and soon all were busy with the arrangements for the celebration the following day. A local lumbering company had provided three lumber-floored boweries for afternoon concerts and evening dances. Captain Ballo's band, the Nauvoo Brass Band, and bands from Springville, Ogden, and Salt Lake City played throughout the day. Several units of the Nauvoo Legion lent a military touch to the celebration." Eugene Campbell, *Establishing Zion: The Mormon Church in the American West, 1847–1869* (Salt Lake City: Signature Books, 2009), 236–237.

20. "The 24ᵗʰ of July in the Tops of the Mountains," *Deseret News,* July 29, 1857; Orson Hyde, in *Journal of Discourses* (London: Latter-day Saints Book Depot, 1854–86), 6:12. A 20 August 1857 Brigham Young Office Journal entry quotes President Young as stating: "The day I entered Salt Lake Valley 24 July 1847 I remarked—If the devil will let us alone for ten years, we will bid them defiance. July 24 1857—10 years to a day—I first heard of the intended expedition to Utah under General Harney," in *The Complete Discourses of Brigham Young,* 3:1323.

21. Brigham Young, Remarks at the Salt Lake City Bowery, 16 August 1857, in *The Complete Discourses of Brigham Young,* 3:1315.

22. "Remarks by Pres. Heber C. Kimball, Bowery, July 26, 1857," *Deseret News,* 5 August 1857. Spelling standardized. Excerpts from Heber C. Kimball's 19 July 1857 comments were reprinted in Eastern newspapers. See, for example, "From Washington," *New York Times,* October 1, 1857.

23. Although popularly known as the Utah War, it was not a war in the traditional sense. There were no pitched battles and no casualties due to military combat. As historian William P. MacKinnon has pointed out, however, it was not a bloodless conflict. The largest death toll associated with the conflict occurred on 11 September 1857 at Mountain Meadows

in southern Utah Territory when Mormon vigilantes and local Indians attacked a wagon train of settlers bound for California killing more than one hundred men, women, and children. The most thorough investigation of that tragedy is Ronald W. Walker, Richard E. Turley Jr., and Glen M. Leonard, *Massacre at Mountain Meadows: An American Tragedy* (New York: Oxford University Press, 2008). See also "The Utah Expedition," *Message from the President of the United States, Transmitting Reports from the Secretaries of State, of War, of the Interior, and of the Attorney General, relative to the military expedition ordered into the Territory of Utah*, Ex. Doc. No. 71, 35th Congress, 1st Session (Washington, DC: House of Representatives, 1858).

24 During a morning meeting, Brigham Young noted that "Captain Van Vliet visited us in Winter Quarters. . . . He has always been found to be free and frank, and to be a man that wishes to do right. . . . Many of you have laboured for him, and found him to be a kind, good man. . . ." That afternoon Young told his listeners that "Capt Van Vliet said that if Our Government pushed forward this thing & made war upon us He should withdraw from the army for he would not have a hand in shedding the blood of American Citizens." Remarks at the Salt Lake Bowery, 13 September 1857, in *The Complete Discourses of Brigham Young*, 3:1334, 1342. Spelling standardized.

25 Brigham Young, Remarks at the Salt Lake City Bowery, 13 September 1857, in *The Complete Discourses of Brigham Young*, 3:1336.

26 Wilford Woodruff Journal, ed. Scott G. Kinney, *Wilford Woodruff's Journal: 1833–1898*, 9 typescript vols. (Salt Lake City: Signature Books, 1983), 5:96–97.

27 "Sermon," *Deseret News*, 23 September 1857.

28 Capt. Jesse A. Gove to Maria Gove, October 1857, quoted in LeRoy R. Hafen and Ann W. Hafen, *Mormon Resistance: A Documentary Account of the Utah Expedition, 1857–1858* (Lincoln, NE: University of Nebraska, 1958), 88.

29 See Walker, Turley, and Leonard, *Massacre at Mountain Meadows*.

30 B. H. Roberts, *A Comprehensive History of The Church of Jesus Christ of Latter-day Saints*, 6 vols. (Provo, UT: Brigham Young University Press, 1965), 4:273–274.

31 Brigham Young, Remarks at the Salt Lake City Bowery, 13 September 1857, in *The Complete Discourses of Brigham Young*, 3:1336.

32 Daniel Hanmer Wells replaced Jedediah M. Grant as Second Counselor in the First Presidency earlier in 1857. "Young was fond of saying Heber was the prophet and Wells his statesman. A craggy, full-maned, Lincolnesque figure, with jutting chin whiskers and a cast eye, Wells had been a pre-Mormon resident of Nauvoo. He joined the church in 1846 and during the 1848 trek west served as Young's aide-de-camp. . . . In Utah, before becoming a member of the First Presidency, Wells served in the territorial legislature, as attorney general of the State of Deseret, major general of the militia, superintendent of church public works, and member of the city council." Stanley B. Kimball, *Heber C. Kimball: Mormon Patriarch and Pioneer* (Champaign, IL: University of Illinois Press, 1986), 212.

33 MacKinnon, *At Sword's Point, Part 1,* 321.

34 As quoted in Edward W. Tullidge, *The History of Salt Lake City and Its Founders* (Salt Lake City: By the Author, 1886), 172.

35 Norman F. Furniss, *The Mormon Conflict: 1850–1859* (New Haven, CT: Yale University Press, 1960), 116, 144; B. H. Roberts, *Comprehensive History of the Church*, 4:283–85.

36 Henry S. Hamilton, *Reminiscences of a Veteran* (Concord, NH: Republican Press Association, 1897), 80.

37 "Narrative of Lot Smith," in Hafen and Hafen, *Mormon Resistance*, 222.

38 Brigham Young, Remarks in Salt Lake City, 16 January 1858, in *The Complete Discourses of Brigham Young*, 3:1397.

39 Brigham Young, Remarks in Salt Lake City, 28 February 1858, *The Complete Discourses of Brigham Young*, 3:1411.

40 Thomas G. Alexander, *Things in Heaven and Earth: The Life and Times of Wilford Woodruff, a Mormon Prophet* (Salt Lake City: Signature Books, 1993), 175.

41 Leonard J. Arrington, "Mormon Finance and the Utah War," *Utah Historical Quarterly*, Vol. 20 (1952), 219.

42 "Affairs at the National Capital," *New York Daily Times*, 1 June 1857.

43 Fort Supply was twelve miles from Fort Bridger in present-day southwest Wyoming. See Fred R. Gowans and Eugene E. Campbell, *Fort Bridger: Island in the Wilderness* (Provo, UT: Brigham Young University Press, 1975), 91.

44 "President's Message," *New York Times*, 7 December 1858.

45 "XXXVth Congress . . . First Session," *New York Times*, 27 January 1858.

46 "The Ocean Mail Service," *New York Times*, 7 May 1858; "The Pacific Railroad—Its Effects upon Commerce Christianity and Civilization," *New York Times*, 29 December 1858.

47 "Latest Intelligence," *New York Times*, 7 April 1858.

48 "Important from Washington," *New York Times*, 11 June 1858.

49 During 1857–1858, there were approximately 2,200 *New York Daily Times* and *New York Times* articles regarding Kansas and slavery and 1,200 articles pertaining to Utah and the Mormons (based on research conducted by the author).

50 "The Mormons," *New York Times*, 17 October 1857.

51 "The Utah Expedition," *New York Times*, 14 December 1857; "News of the Day," *New York Times*, 8 January 1858.

52 "Horrible Rumor from the Plains," *New York Times*, 8 January 1858.

53 "Latest by Telegraph," *New York Times*, 5 May 1858.

54 "The Last News from Utah," *New York Times*, 21 May 1858.

55  "Are the Mormons in Rebellion?" *New York Times*, 23 January 1858.

56  Prince Gortschakoff, the Russian general commanding Sebastopol (which is also sometimes alternatively spelled "Sevastopol"), "felt that it would be impossible for him to hold the city much longer, and that to remain there was only useless waste of life," so he ordered the city to be burned. In the dispatch recounting his decision, he stated, "It is not Sebastopol which we have left to them, but the burning ruins of the town, which we ourselves set fire to, having maintained the honour of the defence in such a manner that our great grandchildren may recall with pride the remembrance of it and send it on to all posterity." Justin McCarthy, *A History of Our Own Times from the Accession of Queen Victoria to the General Election of 1880*, 5 vols. (New York: Frederick A. Stokes Company, 1890), 2:257.

57  Brigham Young, Unpublished Discourse, August 16, 1857, LDS Archives, in MacKinnon, *Sword's Point*, 239–243.

58  Wilford Woodruff Journal, 5;177

59  Ibid. Spelling standardized.

60  Brigham Young, Remarks in the Salt Lake Tabernacle, 21 March 1858, in *The Complete Discourses of Brigham Young*, 3:1416, 1420.

61  Brigham Young, Remarks in Salt Lake Tabernacle, 21 March 1858, in *The Complete Discourses of Brigham Young*, 3:1414, 1417, 1420.

62  Wilford Woodruff Journal, 5:178. Spelling standardized.

63  Richard D. Poll, "The Move South," *BYU Studies* 29·4 (Fall 1989), 71.

64  Andrew Jackson Allen Journal, in Joel E. Ricks Collection of Transcriptions, Vol. 1, MS 82,37, Church History Library, Salt Lake City.

65  Poll, "The Move South," 80.

66  Kate Carter, *Our Pioneer Heritage*, 20 vols. (Salt Lake City: Daughters of Utah Pioneers, 1958–1977), 2:9.

67  Wilford Woodruff Journal, 5:178. Spelling standardized.

68  Poll, "The Move South," 72.

69  Brigham Young had publicly discussed "Cashing" [burying] the temple foundation as early as 16 August 1857. *Journal History of the Church*, March 25, 1858, in *The Complete Discourses of Brigham Young*, 3:1322.

70  Poll, "The Move South," 74.

71  G. R., quoted in Kate Carter, *Our Pioneer Heritage*, 2:10–11.

72  History of Joseph C. Kingsbury, *New Mormon Studies CD-ROM: A Comprehensive Resource Library* (Salt Lake City: Signature Books, 2009).

73  "The Mormons," *New York Times*, June 25, 1858; "Latest Intelligence," *New York Daily Times*, May 18, 1857; "Arrival of the Star of the West," *New York Times*, October 5, 1857; "Latest Intelligence," *New York Times*, November 20, 1857; "From Washington," *New York Times*, November 25, 1857; "Letter from an Officer of the Utah Expedition," *New York Times*, November 26, 1857; "News of the Day," *New York Times*, January 13, 1858; "The Lecomptonites Flurried—Probable Compromise, &c," *New York Times*, February 5, 1858; "Government and the Mormons—One of the Herald's Stories Exploded," *New York Times*, February 6, 1858; "The Future Home of the Mormons," *New York Times*, February 10, 1858; "The Last News from Utah," *New York Times*, May 21, 1858; "News of the Day," *New York Times*, June 16, 1858; No Title, *New York Times*, June 22, 1858; and "The Mormons," *New York Times*, June 25, 1858.

74  "Late and Important from the Utah Expedition," *New York Times*, January 16, 1858.

75  "News of the Day," *New York Times*, June 10, 1858.

76  Published estimates for the number of participants in the Move South range from 30,000 to 80,000. It should be noted that the 1860 federal census counted Utah's population as 40,273. See Campbell, *Establishing Zion*, 248–249; William G. Hartley, "The Miller, the Bishop, and the 'Move South,'" *BYU Studies* 20:1 (Fall 1979); and Orson F. Whitney, *Life of Heber C. Kimball* (Salt Lake City: Deseret Book, 2001), 415–416.

77  Clifford L. Stott, *Search for Sanctuary: Brigham Young and the White Mountain Expedition* (Salt Lake City: University of Utah Press, 1984), 67.

78  When Bean was eighteen, a major accident "changed his life forever. During a military exercise at the fort [Fort Utah, later Provo], a cannon exploded sending hundreds of wood and iron fragments into his body. His left arm was shattered and had to be amputated 3½ inches below the elbow which, according to Bean, 'left a useful stub.'" While he recuperated, he spent his time studying Indian languages and became fluent in Ute. Stott, *Search for Sanctuary*, 67–68.

79  Dame had known Brigham Young since Nauvoo. In 1851 he was called to settle Utah's Iron County. Thirty-eight years old and a colonel in the Nauvoo Legion, Dame served several terms in the territorial legislature immediately prior to the Utah War. Stott, *Search for Sanctuary*, 85–87.

80  Lorenzo also remembered that "we took no chickens with us, but our neighbor, whose name was Flint, had quite a flock. One day a small speckled hen wandered over to see us, descended our steps, strolled through the open doorway, and chose to lay an egg on my mother's bed. We took it over to Brother Flint's and explained what had happened. To my surprise he sent it back again in a most friendly manner." Lorenzo S. Clark Journal, in Kate B. Carter, *Heart Throbs of the West*, Vol. 9 (Salt Lake City: Daughters of Utah Pioneers, 1948), 391–392.

81  Mary Ann Young to Robert L. Campbell, March 23, 1857, *Journal History of the Church*. Accessed electronically, Richard E. Turley, Jr., ed., *Selected Collections from the Archives of the Church of Jesus Christ of Latter-day Saints*, Vol. 2 (Provo, UT: Brigham Young University Press, 2002).

82  Friday, April 30, 1857, *Journal History of the Church*.

83  Andrew Jackson Allen Journal, MS837. Spelling standardized.

84  Wilford Woodruff Journal, 5:183, 185. Spelling standardized.

85  A. Cumming to B. Young, 18 May 1858, *Journal History of the Church*.

86   27 May 1858, *Journal History of the Church*.

87   30 May 1858, *Journal History of the Church*.

88   "The Mormon Exodus," *New York Times*, 17 June 1858.

89   Thomas L. Kane, "Concerning the Mormons and Pres. Buchanan," July 1858, Kane Papers, American Philosophical Society, in MacKinnon, *At Sword's Point, Part I*, 495.

90   Thomas L. Kane, "Concerning the Mormons," in MacKinnon, *At Sword's Point, Part I*, 495. "I had to convince his [Buchanan's] reason why I must refuse an appointment from him, by showing him how important it was that I could be warranted in assuring the Mormons that I was not a Government agent. . . . In a letter he [Buchanan] wrote for me he stated this at my request."

91   Wilford Woodruff's Journal, 5:168. Spelling standardized.

92   Wilford Woodruff's Journal, Vol. 5, 169. While in Utah, Kane received news of his father's death. See 4 May 1858, *Journal History of the Church*. Spelling standardized.

93   Thursday, April 8, 1857, *Journal History of the Church*.

94   A. Cumming to A. S. Johnston, April 15, 1858, in Orson F. Whitney, *History of Utah*, 4 vols. (Salt Lake City: George Q. Cannon & Sons Co., 1892), 1:673.

95   Hubert Howe Bancroft, *History of Utah* (Salt Lake City: Bookcraft, 1964), 531.

96   Wilford Woodruff Journal, 5:195. Spelling standardized.

97   Brigham Young, Remarks in Provo, Utah, 12 June 1858, in *Journal History of the Church*, March 25, 1858, in *The Complete Discourses of Brigham Young*, 3:440.

98   Hope A. Hilton, *"Wild Bill" Hickman and the Mormon Frontier* (Salt Lake City: Signature Books, 1988), 80.

99   Ray R. Canning and Beverly Beeton, eds., *The Genteel Gentile: Letters of Elizabeth Cumming, 1857–1858* (Salt Lake City: University of Utah Tanner Trust Fund, 1977), 81.

100  Randolph Barnes Marcy, *Thirty Years of Army Life on the Border* (Bedford, MA: Applewood Books, n.d.), 264.

101  Leo J. Muir, ed., *The Life Story of George William McCune including His Forebears, Immediate Kinsfolk and Posterity* (Los Angeles: Westernlore Press, 1959), 65. McCune's autobiography was originally published in *Utah Genealogical Magazine,* October 1925. On the previous page, McCune incorrectly dated the date of the army's march through Salt Lake City as 3 June 1858.

102  Quoted in Averam B. Bender, *The March of Empire: Frontier Defense in the Southwest 1848–1860* (Lawrence, Kansas: University of Kansas Press, 1952), 183–184.

103  Asa S. Hawley Journal, MS 2050, Box 3, Folder 7, Church History Library, Salt Lake City.

104  Andrew Jackson Allen Journal, MS 8237. Spelling standardized.

105  Jean Baker, "Gathering to Zion" in Arrington and Bitton, *Saints Without Halos: The Human Side of Mormon History* (Salt Lake City: Signature Books, 1981), 46.

106  Brigham Young, Remarks at the Bowery, 13 September 1857, in *The Complete Discourses of Brigham Young*, 3:1339.

107  Stanley B. Kimball, *Heber C. Kimball*, 260.

108  Hope Hilton, *"Wild Bill" Hickman*, 68.

109  Rebecca Bartholomew, *Audacious Women: Early British Mormon Immigrants* (Salt Lake City: Signature Books, 1995), 99.

110  Brigham Young, Remarks at the Salt Lake Bowery, 13 September 1857, in *The Complete Discourses of Brigham Young*, 3:1337.

111  Alexander, *Things in Heaven and Earth*, 198–199.

112  "Light Wanted on the Mormon Difficulty," *New York Times*, 28 January 1858. Concerns over granting statehood to Utah Territory remained after the Utah War. For an examination of Utah Territory statehood discussions during the Civil War, see Kenneth L. Alford, "Utah and the Civil War Press," *Utah Historical Quarterly* 80:1 (Winter 2012): 75–92.

113  "Affairs in Utah," *New York Times*, November 27, 1865.

114  See William P. MacKinnon, "Prelude to Civil War: The Utah War's Impact and Legacy," in Kenneth L. Alford, ed., *Civil War Saints* (Provo, UT: Brigham Young University Religious Studies Center and Deseret Book, 2012).

115  "Unfair Treatment of Utah," *Deseret News,* 2 June 1858. Spelling standardized.

116  "The Mormon Exodus," *New York Times*, 17 June 1858.

117  Wilford Woodruff Journal, 5:89–91. Spelling standardized.

118  George A. Smith, in *Journal of Discourses* (London: Latter-day Saints Book Depot, 1854–86), 9:19.

119  "Cruel Panegyrics of the Administration Press," *New York Times*, 23 June 1858. Italics in original.

120  "The Mormon Exodus," *New York Times*, 17 June 1858.

121  Lemuel Fillmore, *New York Herald,* 19 July 1858.

122  Kate B. Carter, *Heart Throbs of the West,* 9:258.

123  John Jaques, "The Mormon Question," *Deseret News*, July 21, 1858.

124  8 May 1858, *Journal History of the Church*.

# CHAPTER SIX

# THE WAR ON POLYGAMY

### THOMAS G. ALEXANDER

In the nineteenth century, the practice of polygamy by members of The Church of Jesus Christ of Latter-day Saints evoked vigorous national opposition. The Mormons called it plural marriage, celestial marriage, or just "the Principle," but almost no one but them approved of it.

Protestants ruled the nation during the nineteenth century, and they cursed the practice as immoral. Stories of the Mormon practice of polygamy circulated widely. After Judges Lemuel Brandebury and Perry Brocchus, Territorial Secretary Broughton Harris, and Indian Sub agent Henry Day fled the territory in 1851, they denounced polygamy.

Significantly, when Mormons first heard of it, many of them found it odious as well. After Brigham Young learned of plural marriage, he said that it shook him so deeply that "it was the first time in my life that I had desired the grave, and I could hardly get over it for a long time." Yet he obeyed Joseph Smith's advice, and he eventually married fifty-five women.

Faced with almost universal opposition, the Mormons preached and defended the practice as a religious principle commanded by God. They publicly acknowledged plural marriage in August 1852 when Orson Pratt announced and defended it. Thereafter numerous Mormons spoke or wrote in defense of polygamy. Some, like Joseph F. Smith and George Q. Cannon, argued that Saints had to enter into polygamous

When first taught the doctrine of plural marriage by Joseph Smith, Brigham Young said, "It was the first time in my life that I had desired the grave." However, once converted to the principle, he went on to marry fifty-five women.

Right: Orson Pratt was the man chosen in August 1852 to preach the first public discourse on plural marriage. Ironically, Elder Pratt had struggled mightily with the doctrine when he first learned of it in Nauvoo from the Prophet Joseph Smith.

Right: Orson Pratt—courtesy of the Church History Library

T.F. HEALY COLLECTION

"Mormonism in Utah—the Cave of Despair." An Anti-Mormon Print, Attacking the Former Custom of Bringing Emigrant Girls From Europe, to Be "Sealed" Into Plural Marriages With Mormons.

Polygamy found its way to national consciousness when the Republican Party announced its party platform for the 1856 presidential election to be the abolishment of the "twin relics of barbarism"— slavery and polygamy.

marriages in order to reach the highest degree of the celestial kingdom. Cannon said that he did not feel like sustaining anyone in a Church calling who did not practice plural marriage. Many Mormons argued that the Free Exercise of Religion clause of the US Constitution's First Amendment protected the practice.

After polygamy was publicly announced, national leaders denounced it. In 1856, opposition became solidly entrenched in national politics. The newly formed Republican Party proclaimed its firm opposition by linking polygamy and slavery as the "twin relics of barbarism."

After the Republicans elected majorities in both houses of Congress and Republican President Abraham Lincoln sat in the White House, they outlawed both of the relics in the territories. In 1862, Congress prohibited slavery and polygamy in the territories because the federal government exercised plenary power over them under the Constitution's property clause, Article 4, section 3.[1]

Congress outlawed polygamy in the territories by approving the Morrill Anti-bigamy Act. This act declared polygamy a felony and prescribed a sentence of five years, a fine of $500, or both for anyone in the territories who married more than one woman. It also dis-incorporated The Church of Jesus Christ of Latter-day Saints and prohibited any religious organization from owning more than $50,000 worth of property in any territory.[2]

During the 1870s and afterward, various Congressmen and Senators proposed additional anti-Mormon legislation. As a friend of the Mormons, Pennsylvania reformer Thomas L. Kane worked with Utah territorial delegates and friendly Congressmen and Senators to defeat or amend this legislation. Kane initiated a lobbying effort that reached various members of Congress and US presidents to try to defeat anti-Mormon legislation. He became even more intensely involved in Mormon relations with the federal government following President Ulysses S. Grant's 1870 appointment of James B. McKean as Chief Justice of the Utah Territorial Supreme Court.[3]

Born in Vermont, McKean had moved to New York, served as a county judge, fought in the Civil War, and entered private legal practice in New York City. Grant appointed him to the Utah court reportedly on the recommendation of his friend, the Reverend John P. Newman, a Methodist bishop and chaplain of the United States Senate.[4]

In 1872, while in Washington, McKean reflected on two years of service. In conversation with Grant's brother-in-law and Julia Dent Grant's brother, Louis Dent, McKean said that he had gone on a mission from God to suppress Mormonism.[5]

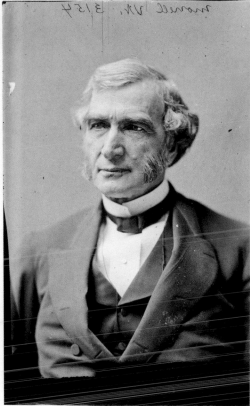

Sen. Justin Smith Morrill of Vermont, sponsor of the Morrill Anti-bigamy Act. The Morrill Anti-bigamy Act was the first law against polygamy in the Utah Territory. Passed in the summer of 1862 as the Civil War was heating up, it made polygamy a felony.

Grant undoubtedly shared McKean's views on the need to suppress Mormon polygamy and to control theocratic government. His appointment of anti-Mormon judges Cyrus M. Hawley, Obed F. Strickland, and Jacob S. Boreman reflected those feelings. In Utah, US Attorney for Utah William Carey and his assistant, Robert N. Baskin, both hated the Mormons intensely. On the other hand, some of Grant's appointees—such as Territorial Secretary Samuel A. Mann, Judge Philip H. Emerson, and US attorneys George C. Bates and Sumner Howard—tried to work with the Mormons.[6]

In Utah, Mormons controlled the selection of juries. Under the Utah Judiciary Act of 1852, the county probate court judges selected the jury pool from lists of property owners. In order to subvert the probate judges' power of jury selection, McKean devised an illegal tactic to remove all Mormons from grand and eventually from trial juries. Ruling that territorial courts were United States district courts, he said that the courts need not follow territorial law in empaneling juries. He then authorized the US marshal to empanel grand juries on an open venire rather than having the probate judge select them from the tax rolls. Under McKean's ruling, the marshal

simply went out on the street and picked men to serve on the grand jury. Not surprisingly, he chose only non-Mormons for jury service. This led to juries packed with anti-Mormons who returned indictments against prominent Mormons.[7]

Instead of securing indictments for polygamy under the Morrill Act, however, McKean had the marshal empanel an anti-Mormon grand jury that indicted Mormon leaders Brigham Young, George Q. Cannon, and Daniel H. Wells and Godbeite leader Henry W. Lawrence under territorial law that prohibited lewd and lascivious cohabitation and adultery.[8] After admitting Brigham Young to $5,000 bail, McKean denied the motion to quash the indictment by Young's attorney, Thomas Fitch. In a long statement of his intent, McKean asserted that although "the case at bar is called, '*The People versus Brigham Young*,' its other and real title is, '*Federal Authority versus Polygamic Theocracy*.'" [9]

James McKean was appointed in 1870 by US President Ulysses S. Grant as chief justice of the Utah Territorial Supreme Court. He was among those federal appointees who hated the Mormons and did all in his power to harass them.

Thomas Fitch was the attorney chosen to defend President Brigham Young against the indictments prosecuted by Judge James McKean.

Fitch filed a bill of exceptions to McKean's outrageous pronouncement. Clearly, as Orma Linford has argued, McKean had perverted the territorial law's intent because "the Mormons [through the Utah legislature] had not intended the adultery and lewd and lascivious cohabitation laws to apply to their plural marriage system." To add insult to injury, McKean refused to recognize the marriage exception to the testimony of wives against their husbands.[10]

After learning what McKean had done, a number of prominent non-Mormons found McKean's ruling outrageous as well. Among those were Patrick Edward Connor, who had previously established Fort Douglas and had condemned the Mormons, and the Walker Brothers, who had left the LDS Church because of disputes over economic policy. US Attorney George C. Bates, who had to prosecute the accused, questioned the indictments because he could not understand why the grand jury did not indict the Mormon leaders under the Morrill Act, which prohibited polygamy, rather than under local laws that the territorial legislature had passed to punish adultery and prostitution rather than plural marriage.[11]

Anxious to proceed in spite of this opposition, in October 1871 McKean started excluding all Mormons from trial juries as well as grand juries. He did this by removing from jury pools those who believed in the revelation authorizing plural marriage, regardless of whether they practiced it. Young recognized that McKean's action placed him and other Church leaders in jeopardy, and he turned to Kane for help. Fearful of trusting the United States mail, Young sent his son John W. Young to Kane with a letter pleading for assistance. McKean's rulings, he wrote, "have deprived the old settlers here of the right to sit on all juries, and in other ways deny to us the rights belonging to the common people." He believed that McKean and his associates "have at last succeeded in what they trust will be a death blow to Mormonism."[12]

The letter also apprised their friend of the danger created by this and other actions by McKean. In a letter replying to Young, Kane said that he considered coming to Utah to meet with the prophet, which he eventually did during the winter of 1872–1873. In the meantime, in view of the indictment, he advised Young to hire William M. Evarts as his attorney. Evarts had served as chief counsel for Andrew Johnson in his impeachment trial and as US attorney general during the early years of the Grant administration.[13]

Fearing for Young's life under McKean's judicial reign of terror, Kane suggested that the prophet hide out and restrict information on his location to close friends. He gave the advice, he wrote, because "in the present crisis, I can think of nothing as essential to the safety of your people as your personal security." In addition, he

John W. Young, the son of President Brigham Young, was entrusted with this letter, summoning the help of Colonel Thomas L. Kane. President Young hoped Colonel Kane would aid and assist the Saints in battling the illegal prosecutions of Judge James McKean.

Kane, Octr. 12./71

Dear and honored old friend:

Your letter of the 27.th ult. has received
due attention, as your son who bears this
will acquaint you. I trust the particulars
communicated by him will much relieve your
mind. He will tell you I am not the
only American Citizen who deems it patriotic
to do right.

But, though the blow immediately
threatening has, as far as we can judge, been
parried, I must solicit you to give me the
benefit of your views meditations upon the
future. Your people never stood more in
need of Statesmanship. We must lead
and direct events, or bad men will.

You must retain the best legal counsel

President Young.

In the manner of a true friend, Thomas Kane wrote back to Brigham Young and promised his assistance. Among other things, he advised Brigham Young to go into hiding, adding, "I can think of nothing as essential to the safety of your people as your personal security."

suggested that George A. Smith, John Taylor, Orson Pratt, and other prominent leaders go into hiding as well. "We do not want," he wrote, "your persecutors to get hold of anyone with name enough to help them to a sensational trial."[14]

Instead of hiding, however, Young turned himself in. McKean refused to admit him to bail, but because of Young's ill health, the judge sentenced him to house arrest rather than incarcerating him at Fort Douglas with some of the others whom the grand jury had indicted.[15]

After learning of Young's arrest, Kane began lobbying for McKean's removal. He met with various Congressman and with Grant, hoping to provide legislative relief or to remove McKean and his supporters from office. He pointed out that Young's California friends had agreed to serve as sureties for bail equal to a hundred times that accepted for Jefferson Davis, a traitor and the former president of the Confederacy. Kane and other friends, including Pennsylvania Senator Simon Cameron, met with leaders like Grant and Secretary of State Hamilton Fish to try to convince them to try to stop McKean's judicial crusade. Instead of helping him, however, Grant seemed bent on prosecuting Young.[16]

After Young had spent several months under house arrest while other accused polygamists remained at Fort Douglas, the United States Supreme Court ruled against McKean. In a decision that forced McKean to retreat, the Supreme Court ruled in 1872 in *Clinton* v. *Englebrecht* that the territorial federal courts had to follow Utah law in empaneling juries.[17] The decision forced McKean to throw out 130 illegal indictments his packed juries had delivered, including those against Young, Cannon, Wells, and Lawrence, and it vacated those judgments returned by his illegal trial juries as well.[18]

Thwarted in his efforts to try the Mormons for lewd and lascivious cohabitation, McKean found in 1873 an additional way to harass Young. McKean accepted the divorce suit of Ann Eliza Webb Dee Young, one of Young's polygamous wives. Failing to recognize that Young's marriage to Ann Eliza was illegal under the Morrill Act, McKean ordered the prophet to pay alimony of $500 per month pending the outcome of the litigation. Young refused to do so on the ground that he was legally married to Mary Ann Angell. He argued that Ann Eliza had been sealed to him in a religious ceremony, not a legal marriage. Refusing to accept Young's argument, McKean fined him $25 and sent him to the territorial penitentiary in Sugar House for a night. Recognizing that ruling the marriage as legitimate would undermine federal statutes that prohibited polygamy, the US attorney general later ordered the case dismissed.[19]

In the meantime, anti-Mormons in Congress had proposed additional legislation to attack the Latter-day Saints. Ohio Senator Benjamin Wade in 1866 and Senator Aaron Cragin of New Hampshire in 1868 introduced bills that would have eliminated local government in Utah. In 1870 Illinois Congressman Shelby M. Cullom introduced a bill to exclude all believers in polygamy from juries, to allow wives to testify against their husbands, and to prohibit polygamists from voting or holding office.[20] Ohio Congressman James Ashley proposed to dismember Utah by assigning all but a narrow strip of land to Nevada, Wyoming, and Colorado.[21]

After the failure of McKean's judicial crusade, Kane continued to work for the Mormons on a number of other matters. He helped, for instance, to mitigate the impact of the Poland Act of 1874[22] introduced by Congressman Luke P. Poland of Vermont. Kane also tried unsuccessfully to derail the Edmunds Act of 1882.[23]

In spite of persuasive lobbying to remove Judge James McKean and halt his crusade against the Mormons, President Ulysses S. Grant (above) sustained Judge McKean and his prosecutions.

Ann Eliza Young, a plural wife of Brigham Young, sued him for divorce. In accepting the case, Judge James McKean had to acknowledge the validity of plural marriage in order to prosecute the case. Judge McKean proceeded with the case notwithstanding the contradictions. The case was later thrown out, but not before President Young was fined $25 and spent a night in the territorial penitentiary.

The Poland Act made a number of judicial and administrative changes in Utah. Henceforth, the clerk of the US district court, usually a non-Mormon, selected half of the jury pool; the other half was selected by the judge of the county probate court, generally a Mormon. The act abolished the offices of territorial marshal and attorney, most of whom were Mormons, and placed their duties in the hands of the US marshal and attorney, usually non-Mormon federal appointees. The act also abolished the civil and criminal jurisdiction of the county probate courts and vested exclusive jurisdiction over these matters to the US district courts.

The crusade against the Mormons continued unabated. After the passage of the Poland Act, the federal judges and attorneys began to prosecute unrepentant polygamists under the Morrill Act. George Reynolds, one of Brigham Young's clerks, agreed to stand trial to test the constitutionality of the Morrill Act.

In the first of two trials, Reynolds's second wife, Amelia Jane Schofield Reynolds, testified that she had married Reynolds as a plural wife. Because of her testimony, the jury brought a guilty verdict. Reynolds appealed his conviction on a technicality, and the Utah Territorial Supreme Court overturned his conviction.

Although Reynolds had agreed to stand as a test case in the first trial, he most likely did not in the second. In the second

George Reynolds, a clerk and secretary for the First Presidency, agreed to present evidence sufficient to convict him of polygamy under the Morrill Anti-bigamy Act. This case would eventually make its way to the United States Supreme Court. The court upheld Reynolds's conviction, thereby establishing the precedent for interpretation of the First Amendment's free exercise of religion clause.

trial, federal officials could not find Amelia Jane. In her absence, the judge authorized the prosecution to introduce her testimony from the first trial. The jury returned a guilty verdict, and the judge sentenced Reynolds to pay $500 and serve two years at hard labor.

After appealing unsuccessfully to the Utah Territorial Supreme Court, Reynolds appealed to the United States Supreme Court. In a decision written by Chief Justice Morrison Waite, the court sustained Reynolds's conviction. Significantly, Waite's decision has formed the basic interpretation of the First Amendment's free exercise of religion clause since that time. In his ruling, Waite wrote that you could believe anything you wished, but that the law could punish actions that "were in viola-tion of social duties or subversive of good order." Laws, the court said, governed actions, and that while they might not "interfere with mere religious belief and opinions, they may with practices." Reynolds had married two women while Western civilization had generally approved the marriage of one man and one woman. In a subsequent hearing, the court did overturn the sentence to hard labor but affirmed his two-year incarceration.[24]

Reynolds's conviction, however, proved an illusory victory for anti-polygamists, since a ruling in a subsequent case made the Morrill Act difficult to enforce. In the case of *United States* v. *Miles* (1880), the court ruled that prosecutors had to provide legal evidence of the second marriage. Courts could not assume such a marriage occurred, nor could they require a wife to testify against her husband. In this case, Caroline "Carrie" Owens Miles agreed to marry John Miles if he married her as his first wife. When Caroline learned that John had married Emily Spencer Miles first, she approached the US marshal and agreed to testify against her husband. In response, John testified that Caroline was his wife, but he denied he had married Emily. Utah had no civil registration at the time, but in spite of Miles's testimony that Caroline was his wife, the trial court admitted her testimony that she was a polyga-mous wife. The US Supreme Court overturned the lower court ruling on the ground that the prosecution had not proved that a polygamous marriage had taken place. The Supreme Court ruled that "until the fact of the marriage of Emily Spencer with the plaintiff in error was estab-lished, Caroline Owens was prima facie his wife, and she could not be used as a witness against him." This ruling made proof of subse-quent marriages almost impossible to find until the Edmunds-Tucker Act of 1887 revoked the law that a wife could not testify against her husband and required Utah Territory to implement civil registration.[25]

After the virtual failure of the Morrill Act to prevent polyga-mous marriages, various Congressmen and Senators introduced additional legislation, and various presidents urged them to act. In messages to Congress, Presidents Ulysses S. Grant, Rutherford B. Hayes, and Chester A. Arthur each called on Congress to pass legislation that would wipe out the practice. In response, Congress passed the Edmunds Act in March 1882, which served as an effec-tive vehicle for prosecuting polygamists.[26] Introduced by Senator George Edmunds of Vermont, the act reiterated the offense of the

John Miles was a polygamist whose case was brought before the United States Supreme Court in 1880. In this instance, the high court dealt a blow to the anti-polygamy crusade when it ruled that a polygamous marriage had to be proven and not just assumed by the prosecution.

felony of bigamy from the Morrill Act. It also defined unlawful cohabitation as a misdemeanor, punishable by six months in prison, a fine of $300, or both. With the passage of the Edmunds Act, the US attorney had to prove only that men and women lived together or, under a loose interpretation accepted by the courts, that they presented themselves to the public as married to each other. The prosecution did not have to provide evidence that an illegal marriage had taken place as it did under the Morrill Act.

The Edmunds Act also contained other features that attacked the Mormon community directly. The act disfranchised all polygamists, declared them ineligible to hold public office, and excused jury candidates who either practiced or believed in polygamy. In addition, the act turned the election machinery of Utah territory over to a commission of five men appointed by the president. The Utah Commission, as it was called, established rules for the enforcement of the provision of the Edmunds Act, prohibiting polygamists from holding office and voting. Commission members appointed the election officers in each of Utah's counties, most of whom were non-Mormons.

Under the law, the Utah Commission was supposed to act only until the Utah Legislature could draft a new election law. Because of conflicts between the Mormon-dominated legislature and anti-Mormon governors who held an absolute veto under the Utah Territorial Organic Act, no new law could be enacted. As a result, the Utah Commission continued to control the election machinery until Utah's admission as a state in 1896.

The Utah Commission drafted a test oath that all potential voters or office holders were required to take. The oath required each voter to swear that he was not cohabiting with more than one wife in a marriage relationship. The commission estimated that the test oath disfranchised approximately 12,000 polygamists. The oath also applied to current office holders; a number were removed, including Utah's territorial delegate, George Q. Cannon.

President Chester Arthur selected Charles S. Zane to serve as the chief justice of the Utah Territorial

In March 1882, Congress passed the Edmunds Act, which was introduced by Vermont Senator George Edmunds. This law allowed for prosecution if a couple simply lived together—a situation that was called "unlawful cohabitation." No marriage had to be proven.

Appointed by the president of the United States, the so-called Utah Commission enforced the provisions of the Edmunds Act, disfranchising Latter-day Saints. This body functioned until 1896, when Utah became a state.

Bottom: The Utah Commission—courtesy of the Church History Library

Supreme Court and as the judge assigned to preside over polygamy cases under the Edmunds Act. A native of New Jersey, Zane moved to Illinois, where he studied law with James C. Conkling, a friend of Abraham Lincoln and William H. Herndon, Lincoln's law partner. After Lincoln left Illinois to assume the presidency, Zane became Herndon's partner. After Herndon retired, Zane partnered with Shelby Cullom until Zane's election as a circuit judge in 1875. A recommendation from Cullom convinced Arthur to appoint Zane in 1884, and Utah Governor Eli H. Murray assigned him to the third judicial district, which covered central Utah, including Salt Lake County.[27]

Zane was, however, of a much different temperament from McKean. Although he came from a Quaker background, Zane was a professed agnostic. Moreover, he held no animosity for the Mormon people but believed he had a duty to enforce the law. Given his attitudes, he did not try to undermine Utah's local laws as McKean had done. Nor did he follow McKean's example of arresting and imprisoning Mormon leaders on spurious charges such as lewd and lascivious cohabitation or murder.

He did, however, insist on the enforcement of the Edmunds Act. Rudger Clawson, a prominent Mormon whose father was a business associate of Brigham Young and who had seen his

Among those disfranchised and ultimately imprisoned under the Edmunds Act was President George Q. Cannon, shown here in the territorial penitentiary.

missionary companion, Joseph Standing, murdered by a mob, tested the constitutionality of the Edmunds Act. The jury returned guilty verdicts for both an illegal marriage and unlawful cohabitation; Zane sentenced Clawson to three and a half years in prison and levied a $1,500 fine. Clawson also failed in his appeal to the US Supreme Court.[28]

During the sentencing, Zane and Clawson exchanged views. Zane said that when "free love, polygamy, or any other system shall be substituted for the monogamic marriage, then this great social fabric which is now protected by law, will probably be crumbling about us; and chastity, virtue and decency, will fall with it." Clawson told Zane that he was sorry that the laws of God had come into conflict with human law. He chose God's law and believed that the Constitution protected him in "perfect freedom to worship God in his own way."[29]

The Edmunds Act and its successor, the Edmunds-Tucker Act, thoroughly disrupted life among the Saints. Among other things, it forced Church leaders into hiding and drove some Church members out of the country.

Because he wanted to uphold the law rather than abuse Mormons, Zane offered lenient sentences to those polygamists who agreed to obey the law. Bishop John Sharp of the Salt Lake 20th Ward, general superintendent of the Utah Central Railroad, was an example. Sharp initially pled not guilty but changed his plea to guilty. Zane could have sentenced him to prison and fined him, but instead he fined Sharp only $300. Following Sharp's guilty plea, the Mormon community ostracized him for a time.[30] Unfortunately, some of those who accepted Zane's leniency could not afford to pay the fine, and they had to serve thirty days in jail in lieu of the fine.[31]

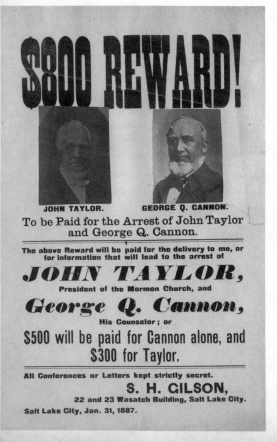

JOHN TAYLOR.     GEORGE Q. CANNON.

To be Paid for the Arrest of John Taylor and George Q. Cannon.

The above Reward will be paid for the delivery to me, or for information that will lead to the arrest of

**JOHN TAYLOR,**

President of the Mormon Church, and

*George Q. Cannon,*

His Counselor ; or

**$500 will be paid for Cannon alone, and $300 for Taylor.**

All Conferences or Letters kept strictly secret.

**S. H. GILSON,**

22 and 23 Wasatch Building, Salt Lake City.

Salt Lake City, Jan. 31, 1887.

Some Mormons tried to find a way to obey the Edmunds Act without giving up polygamy. Angus Cannon, president of the Salt Lake Stake, announced to his families that he intended to support them but intended to obey the law by refraining from sexual intercourse with his wives. The courts, however, refused to accept this solution. The judges interpreted cohabitation to mean that he lived with them or that he "held them out to the world, by his language or conduct, or both, as his wives."[32]

Arrests of prominent Latter-day Saints like Rudger Clawson, John Sharp, and Angus Cannon do not reveal the depths of disruption to the Mormon community caused by the Edmunds Act. Cadres of deputy marshals roamed throughout Mormon communities in Utah, Idaho, and Arizona searching for polygamists. A number of polygamists or polygamous wives went into hiding to try to avoid capture. Wilford Woodruff went to St. George and northern Arizona. Joseph F. Smith fled to San Francisco and Hawaii. George Teasdale scurried to Mexico. John Taylor moved from place to place until his death in Kaysville in 1887.

In a number of cases, deputies arrested both legal and plural wives. The judges pressed these women to testify against their husbands under threat of imprisonment for contempt of court or perjury. A number of them went to prison rather than testify.[33]

In an effort to avoid the reach of American law, a number of polygamous families fled to Mormon colonies in northern Mexico and southwestern Canada. Polygamy was illegal in both countries but Mexico's dictator, Porforio Diaz, liked the progressive attitudes of the Mormons, and he chose not to prosecute the Mormon polygamists. To avoid the reach of Canadian law, where the government did prosecute polygamists, a number of polygamous men left one or more wives in the United States and took another with them to Canada.

Dissatisfied with the assumption that under the Edmunds Act judges could sentence a convict to only six months in prison, the judges proposed a new theory called "segregation." Instead of considering polygamy a continuing offense, Judge Orlando Powers divided it into segments and prosecuted defendants for each segment. In December 1885, Lorenzo Snow, an apostle and leader of the Brigham City community, appeared in Powers's court. The indictment charged Snow with unlawful cohabitation in 1883, 1884, and 1885.

Snow appealed his conviction, arguing that cohabitation constituted a continuing offense. The Utah Territorial Supreme Court upheld the conviction, and Snow could actually have been released from prison before the US Supreme Court finally ruled on his case. The Supreme Court ruled in Snow's favor and the decision forced the Utah federal judges to order his release from prison. As a result of the ruling, judges had to stop arbitrarily dividing what was a continuing offense into separate periods.[34]

In addition to offering amnesty to those who pled guilty, judges like Charles Zane offered a way out of prosecution. William B. Bennett of West Jordan secured a Church divorce from his polygamous wife. The divorce separated the couple for time, but left their sealing for eternity intact. He reported to take the oath in order to vote, but a group of Gentiles objected. They hired former federal

GOVERNOR MURRAY & U.S. OFFICIALS 1884

*1. O.W. Powers, Associate Justice 3d S. W.T.  2. E.H. Ireland, U.S. Marshall, 3d to 4th S.  3. Governor E.H. Murray, 4th S. to Tenth.*
*4. Chas. S. Zane, Chief Justice, 11th S. to 8th.  5. W.H. Dickson, U.S. Atty, 6th to 6th S.  6. J.S. Boreman, Associate Justice, 4th 5th S.*

Judge Powers sought to make the Edmunds Act more onerous for the Latter-day Saints by arbitrarily segmenting unlawful cohabitation from a continuous single offense into multiple offenses. Though successful for a time, this practice was ultimately overruled by the U.S. Supreme Court.

judge Orlando Powers to represent them in Zane's court in a suit against Bennett. In the suit, Powers argued that Bennett and his plural wife were still married for eternity. Siding with Bennett, Zane ruled that a Church divorce was a perfectly legitimate way to comply with the law. Admonishing Powers in court, Zane ruled that opponents should confine discussion "to earthly matters and [leave] the hereafter alone."[35]

In spite of the offers of amnesty, the Edmunds Act had a devastating effect on the Mormon community. Many left their families and occupations to scurry into hiding or to serve terms in prison. In some cases, judges forced unrepentant polygamists to plead guilty by requiring wives to testify or face imprisonment for contempt of court. In total, prosecutions forced more than a thousand men and an uncounted number of women into prison for varying terms.

Throughout all of these trials, Mormons continued to petition to admit Utah into the Union. Utahns drafted constitutions and applied for statehood in 1849, 1856, 1862, 1872, 1882, and 1887 before they finally achieved admission in 1896.[36]

The 1887 attempt came in the middle of Congress's consideration of what is arguably the most punitive piece of legislation in American history aimed at a religious group. As finally passed, the Edmunds-Tucker Act contained provisions for confiscating (the legal term was *escheating*) the property of The Church of Jesus Christ of Latter-day Saints not used exclusively for religious purposes. The law designated the proceeds from the property for the benefit of Utah's public schools. The law also disinherited illegitimate children; disfranchised all women in Utah Territory (they had been able to vote since 1870); required wives to testify against their husbands in polygamy prosecutions; eliminated local election of probate judges; vested the appointment of the territorial commissioner of schools in the territorial supreme court; required

Utah to implement civil registration of marriages; and abolished the territorial militia.[37]

In an attempt to mitigate the impact of the Edmunds-Tucker Act, leaders of the LDS Church sent a committee to Washington to propose a solution. John W. Young, then living in New York, headed the committee until February 1888, when Wilford Woodruff, leading the Church as president of the Quorum of the Twelve Apostles after the death of John Taylor, sent Joseph F. Smith to replace him. A number of other men served on the committee, including three attorneys—Franklin S. Richards, a prominent Mormon, and George Ticknor Curtis and Jeremiah Wilson, both non-Mormons, former federal judges, and constitutional experts.

The committee tried at first unsuccessfully to secure approval of an amendment to the Edmunds-Tucker Act proposed by Congressman William L. Scott of Pennsylvania that would have given Utah six months to include a measure in its constitution prohibiting polygamy. While the effort failed, it probably would have had little effect anyway, because President John Taylor said that although he would approve the amendment he would not give up the practice of polygamy.

After that effort failed, the committee continued to try to get Congress to admit Utah into the Union. Richards, most likely with official approval, testified in the hearings that the practice

Lydia Spencer Clawson (center), the plural wife of Rudger Clawson, was imprisoned under the Edmunds-Tucker Act because she refused to testify against her husband. In other cases, women were forced to testify and their husbands, forced to plead guilty, were subsequently imprisoned.

of polygamy was optional rather than obligatory for Church members. This failed as well.

Two other actions placed Church members in jeopardy as well. Idaho Territory enacted a test oath that barred all believers in polygamy from voting or holding office. Idaho included the provision in its constitution when it was admitted as a state in 1890. The US Supreme Court upheld Idaho's action in *Davis* v. *Beeson* in 1890.[38]

In response to the prosecutions and such cases, Church leadership began to move away from supporting polygamy. After President Taylor's death in 1887, Church leaders asked Church publications like the *Deseret News* and *Salt Lake Herald* to avoid criticizing the federal government and defending polygamy. In 1889 the General Authorities agreed not to preach polygamy and sent word to local leaders to likewise refrain. They reprimanded Elder John W. Taylor, a member of the Quorum of the Twelve Apostles, for doing so at a Juab Stake Conference.[39]

It was not just in Utah that the Latter-day Saints were prosecuted for polygamy. Former federal marshal and later US Senator from Idaho, Fred T. Dubois, was an adamant foe of the Saints. He led the Idaho Territory in enacting a test oath that effectively barred faithful Mormons from voting or holding office.

In 1889, during the Salt Lake City election campaign, Judge Thomas J. Anderson undercut efforts to increase the number of Mormons in the electorate. A group of non-Mormons hired William Dickson and Robert Baskin to oppose the petition of British immigrant John Moore to become an American citizen. The opponents cited statements from the Church's past, including Brigham Young's blood atonement doctrine, a temple oath they called "inimical to the interests of the government," and other anti-government statements. Anderson ruled that Mormons were unfit for citizenship, and the courts began denying naturalization to Mormons.[40]

During the hearings in Judge Anderson's court, the Apostles drafted a response that they published. They denied that the temple oath contained anything "inimical" to the government. They repudiated Brigham Young's preaching of blood atonement, and insisted that they loved the United States.[41] Their efforts had no effect, and all the judges began to deny citizenship to Mormons.

In addition to simply reacting to events, Church leadership moved in positive ways to address their problems. Although Church leadership had found most of its support from the Democratic party, they recognized that in order to achieve statehood they would also need to have the backing of prominent Republicans. In September 1887, Wilford Woodruff met with a number of California Republican politicians and business leaders, including Alexander Badlam, a lapsed Mormon whom he had known in Massachusetts, and Isaac Trumbo, a non-Mormon, major stockholder in a number of Utah mines, and second cousin of Hiram B. Clawson, a prominent Mormon businessman. Through Badlam and Trumbo, Woodruff met with Republican Senator Leland Stanford and other California politicians. Later they met with other Republicans, including Judge Morris Estee, who had chaired the 1888 Republican Convention; James S. Clarkson, chairman of the Republican National Committee in 1891–1892; Secretary of State James G. Blaine; and President Benjamin Harrison.

The Church leadership also appealed to the US Supreme Court on the escheatment of Church property. In a six-to-three decision, the court ruled against the Mormons. Justice Joseph Bradley for the majority said "that the religious and charitable uses intended to be subserved and promoted are the inculcation and spread of the doctrines and usages of the Mormon Church, or Church of Latter-Day Saints, one of the distinguishing features of which is the practice of polygamy,—a crime against the laws, and abhorrent to the sentiments and feelings of the civilized world."[42]

The receiver of Church property, US Marshal Frank H. Dyer, took a number of the Church's secular properties. These included the Gardo House, a massive Second Empire building that served as home for the Church president; the tithing yard, located at the current site of the Joseph Smith Memorial building; and other buildings, farms, and stocks. Church leaders had to pay rent to the federal government to use the confiscated property.

Although Dyer had taken the property, he had developed a rather friendly relationship with some Church leaders. In 1887, he had given Wilford Woodruff—whose first wife, Phebe Carter Woodruff, had died in 1885—what amounted to a free ride by telling him that he knew nothing of the president's family matters.[43] Woodruff managed to live without fear of prosecution after that time.

President Woodruff sought to remedy the Church's pressing problems by actively entering the world of political negotiation. He began meeting with prominent Republicans in order to secure favor toward Utah's quest for statehood and to find some financial relief necessitated by anti-polygamy legislation.

In 1890, however, President Harrison removed Dyer as receiver and appointed Henry W. Lawrence in his place. Lawrence, a leader in the Godbeite movement, had a deep-seated hatred for the Mormons. He had testified against the Church in the John Moore case, and he immediately drafted plans to confiscate the Church's religious properties, including its temples. The Edmunds-Tucker Act had excluded property used exclusively for religious purposes, parsonages, or cemeteries from confiscation. The Supreme Court ruling that emphasized that the Church's tenets were illegal left open the possibility that the receiver might confiscate the Church's temples because they were used for illegal purposes. Lawrence moved immediately to do so by securing a subpoena to force President Woodruff to testify before the grand jury.

Woodruff and George Q. Cannon were touring Mormon settlements in Colorado and New Mexico and the Hawaiian settlement at Iosepa at the time Lawrence secured the subpoena. After they returned, Woodruff avoided service of the subpoena, and he and Cannon traveled to California, where they stayed with Trumbo and met again with a number of political leaders.

On September 21, 1890, Woodruff and Cannon returned from California. Woodruff met with leaders from the St. George Temple on September 22. On September 24 he met with his counselors, those apostles who were in Salt Lake City, and George Reynolds of the First Council of the Seventy. In the meantime, he had worked on drafting the document we call "the Manifesto." On September 25, he announced the Manifesto. In his journal, he wrote that he had "arived at a point in the History of my life as the President of the Church of Jesus Christ of Latter Day saints whare I am under the necessity of acting for the Temporal Salvation of the Church. . . . And after Praying to the Lord & feeling inspired by his spirit I have issued . . . [a ] Proclamation which is sustained by my Councillors and the 12 Apostles." In the Manifesto, he wrote that he "now publicly declair that my advice to the Latter Day Saints is to refrain from Contracting any Marriage forbidden by the Law of the land."[44] On October 6, the membership of the Church accepted the Manifesto in general conference.[45]

Issuance of the Manifesto and its acceptance by the Church membership was the beginning of the end both of sanctioned polygamy in the Church and the war on the Saints over polygamy. Some members still entered polygamy with the approval of Church leaders after 1890, but the number of new marriages declined rapidly.

The practice of polygamy continued to create a stir in the public mind and in the press well into the twentieth century. Many who had entered plural marriage before the Manifesto and those who entered with the approval of some Church leaders afterward continued to live with their wives, but by 1910, general and local leaders in the Church began to try their membership and excommunicate those who entered into new plural marriages. With this barrier removed, most Democrats and Republicans moved beyond previous conditions, and Congress admitted Utah into the Union in 1896.

President Wilford Woodruff issued the Manifesto advising the Latter-day Saints to give up the practice of plural marriage. He was, he said, "under the necessity of acting for the temporal salvation of the Church." The issuance of the Manifesto and subsequent actions by the Church to stop the practice effectively ended the war on polygamy.

# Endnotes

1 Article 4, Section 3 says: "The Congress shall have power to dispose of and make all needful rules and regulations respecting the territory or other property belonging to the United States; and nothing in this Constitution shall be so construed as to prejudice any claims of the United States, or of any particular state."

2 US Statutes at Large, 501.

3 For an article on McKean and his career in Utah, see Thomas G. Alexander, "'Federal Authority versus Polygamic Theocracy:' James B. McKean and the Mormons," *Dialogue: A Journal of Mormon Thought* 1 (Autumn 1966): 85–100. I should point out that I do not now agree with many of the conclusions that I arrived at in defense of McKean. Rather, I now believe that he was an anti-Mormon bigot and that many of his actions were clearly illegal and aimed at undermining Mormonism.

4 Alexander, "'Federal Authority," 85–86.

5 In January 1872, in the Ebbett House in Washington, Judge McKean avowed his principles to Judge Louis Dent, brother-in-law of the president, in these precise words: "Judge Dent, the mission which God has called upon me to perform in Utah, is as much above the duties of other courts and judges as the heavens are above the earth, and whenever or wherever I may find the Local or Federal laws obstructing or interfering therewith, by God's blessing, I shall trample them under my feet." Edward W. Tullidge, *Life of Brigham Young; or, Utah and Her Founders* (New York, 1876), 420–421.

6 On Grant and the people of Utah, see Thomas G. Alexander, "A Conflict of Perceptions: Ulysses S. Grant and the Mormons," *Newsletter of the Ulysses S. Grant Association*, 8 (July 1971): 29–42.

7 Alexander, "'Federal Authority," 86.

8 Alexander, "'Federal Authority," 89.

9 Alexander, "'Federal Authority," 89; Orson F. Whitney, *History of Utah*, 4 vols. (Salt Lake City: George Q. Cannon and Sons, 1892–1904), 2:592; *Salt Lake Tribune,* September 19 and 23, and October 9, 1871.

10 Orma Linford, "The Mormons and the Law: The Polygamy Cases," *Utah Law Review,* 9 (Winter, 1964), 331; 12 *Statutes at Large,* 501; *Salt Lake Tribune,* October 8, 1874; *Friel* v. *Wood,* 1 Hagan (Utah), 160 (1874).

11 Whitney, *History of Utah*, 2:603–605, 620, and 678.

12 Young to Kane, April 16, 1871, Thomas L. Kane Collection, L. Tom Perry Special Collections, Harold B. Library, Brigham Young University, Provo, Utah, box 15, folder 5. (Hereinafter cited as Kane Collection, BYU, with box and folder number.)

13 Kane to Young, October 12, 1871, Kane Collection, BYU, box 15, folder 5; on Evarts, see http://civilwarlandscapes.org/cwla/per/civil/wme/wmef.htm (accessed December 3, 2008).

14 Kane to Young, November 30, 1871, Kane Collection, BYU, box 15, folder 5.

15 Thomas L. Kane, Notes, n.d., probably 1872, Kane Collection, BYU, box 15, folder 5.

16 Thomas L. Kane, Notes, n.d., probably 1872, Kane Collection, BYU, box 15, folder 5; on house arrest, see Grow, "Liberty to the Downtrodden," 615–617.

17 *Clinton* v. *Englebrecht,* 80 US 434, 1872.

18 *Clinton* v. *Englebrecht,* 80 US 434, 1872. On the fallout from this decision, see Cyrus M. Hawley to George H. Williams, November 9, 1872, and McKean to Williams, November 12, 1873, "Department of Justice Selected Documents from the Appointment Clerk Files Relating to Utah Judges," Vol. I, RG 60, National Archives, Washington, DC (Microcopy, Utah State Archives, Salt Lake City); *Salt Lake Tribune,* September 2 and October 5, 1870; October 5, 1871; April 25 and 26, 1872; April 3 and 7, October 22, 23, and 29, and December 10, 1873; and January 3 and 8, February 1, 6, 7, and 12, May 8, June 30, July 23 and 24, and December 19, 1874.

19 Whitney, II, 757–758; *Salt Lake Tribune,* July 31, and August 1 and 29, 1873; July 25 and August 26, 1874; and February 26, 1875.

20 On the Cullom Bill, see Marian Mills Miller, *Great Debates in American History, Civil Rights Part 2,* http://books.google.com/books?id=OQw7AQAAIAAJ&pg=PA439&lpg=PA439&dq=Shelby+Cullom+and+polygamy+legislation&source=bl&ots=MglYx-SxGuI&sig=tfhITOxCLuS3ybYMINGqYNTF-DE&hl=en&sa=X-&ei=fqC3UaiVE5HxiQLw64DADw&ved=0CD0Q6AEwAg#v=onepage&q=Shelby%20Cullom%20and%20polygamy%20legislation&f=false.

21 W. Paul Reeve, "Paper on Congressman James Ashley and the Proposed Dismemberment of Utah," paper presented at the meeting of the Utah State Historical Society, Utah State Capitol Building, September 9, 2010.

22 Statutes at Large, 253.

23 Matthew J. Grow, *Liberty to the Downtrodden: Thomas L. Kane, Romantic Reformer* (New Haven: Yale University Press, 2006), 622, 630, 633, 634, 659–660.

24 Edwin Brown Firmage and Richard Collin Mangrum, *Zion in the Courts: A Legal History of the Church of Jesus Christ of Latter-day Saints, 1830–1900* (Urbana, IL: University of Illinois Press, 1988), 151–156; *Reynolds* v. *United States*, 98 U.S. 145 (1879).

25 Firmage and Mangrum, *Zion in the Courts*, 149–150; *Miles* v. *United States* (103 U.S. 304, 1880).

26 Statutes at Large, 30 (1882).

27 Thomas G. Alexander, "Charles S. Zane: Apostle of the New Era," *Utah Historical Quarterly* 34 (Fall 1966), 292–293.

28 *Clawson* v. *United States*, 113 U.S. 143 (1885).

29 Alexander, "Charles S. Zane," 306–307; http://en.wikipedia.org/wiki/Rudger_Clawson.

30 Alexander, "Charles S. Zane," 307.

31 Sarah Barringer Gordon, "Mormon Polygamy and Criminal Law Enforcement," paper presented at the conference of the Mormon History Association, Layton, Utah, June 7, 2013.

32 Firmage and Mangrum, *Zion in the Courts,* 171.

33 Gordon, "Mormon Polygamy and Criminal Law Enforcement."

34 *Ex Parte Snow*, 120 US 274 (1886).

35 Alexander, "Charles S. Zane," 305.

36 Linda Thatcher, "Struggle for Statehood Chronology," http://historytogo.utah.gov/utah_chapters/statehood_and_the_progressive_era/struggleforstatehoodchronology.html

37 US Statutes at Large, 635 (1887).

38 *Davis* v. *Beeson*, 133 US 333 (1890).

39 Thomas G. Alexander, *Things in Heaven and Earth: The Life and Times of Wilford Woodruff, a Mormon Prophet* (Salt Lake City: Signature Books, 1991), 248, 254.

40 Alexander, *Things in Heaven and Earth*, 254–256.

41 Alexander, *Things in Heaven and Earth*, 257–258.

42 *Late Corporation of the Church of Jesus Christ of Latter-day Saints* v. *United States*, 136 US 1 (May 19, 1890).

43 Alexander, *Things in Heaven and Earth*, 246.

44 Wilford Woodruff, *Wilford Woodruff's Journal, 1833–1898: Typescript*, 9 vols., Scott G. Kenney, ed. (Midvale, Utah: Signature Books, 1983–1985), 9:112–116 (September 22–25, 1890).

45 Woodruff, *Journal*, 9:117 (October 6, 1890).